# TWAYNE'S WORLD LEADERS SERIES

## EDITORS OF THIS VOLUME

Arthur W. Brown
*Bernard M. Baruch College*
*The City University of New York*
and
Thomas S. Knight
*Adelphi University*

## Benjamin Franklin

*New York Public Library Picture Collection*

Benjamin Franklin

# Benjamin Franklin

## By RALPH L. KETCHAM

*Syracuse University*

Twayne Publishers, Inc.   ::   New York

*This Twayne Publishers edition*
*is published by special arrangements with*
*Washington Square Press, Inc.*

ISBN-0-8057-3679-4

To my mother and father, who, like Franklin, agree with Edmund Burke that "all evil requires to triumph in the world is for enough good men to do nothing."

# Contents

# Preface

FROM SOMETIME MIDWAY through Benjamin Franklin's life when he achieved fame as a moralist, civic leader, and scientist, until well into the twentieth century, few doubted his standing as a "great American thinker." Excepting perhaps only Emerson, he was the country's most authentic sage, the fountain of the ideas and outlook thought to be characteristically American. Though a succession of literary critics from Joseph Dennie and Nathaniel Hawthorne to Mark Twain and D. H. Lawrence have persistently debunked his life and thought, to most Americans he was the wise and practical preceptor of his *Autobiography*. As the climate of opinion increasingly reflected modes of thought antithetical to Franklin's, however—positivism in philosophy, behaviorism in social science, relativism in ethics, obscurantism in literature, and specialization in all fields of knowledge—his intellectual stature seemed to diminish. His serene assurance that as reason, common sense, and freedom spread, men would increase steadily in virtue and prosperity seemed more and more superficial and irrelevant. Franklin became either a quaint fossil or a pernicious fraud to many sophisticated students of American thought. But with the publication of Carl Van Doren's great biography in 1938, the brilliant work of Verner W. Crane, I. Bernard Cohen, and others since then, and the enriched view of Franklin apparent in the new edition of his *Papers* undertaken in 1954, acclaim for him has been renewed. Moreover, his new fame presents him neither as a prim thrift-monger nor as a crusading skeptic, but rather finds him a marvelously harmonious and interesting human being who dealt constructively with an amazing range of problems during a long and fruitful life. The present study seeks to interpret his thought in this tradition.

I have included a few footnotes to indicate a special dependence in some instances on others who have written about Franklin's thought. The bibliography records other more general sources for this study. Quotations from Franklin's writings before 1759 are from Leonard W. Labaree and others, eds., *The Papers of Benjamin Franklin* (7 vols., New Haven, 1959——), while those after 1759 are largely from Albert H. Smyth, ed., *The Writings of Benjamin Franklin* (10 vols., New York, 1905-1907). Selections from *The Autobiography of Benjamin Franklin* are from the Yale University Press edition of 1964. Enough is said in the text about each quotation to permit its location in one of those three works. A copy of the manuscript with complete annotation giving a full citation for each of the quotations is on deposit in the Syracuse University Library.

I am indebted to the Yale University Press for permission to reprint Franklin's writings before 1759 from its new and standard edition of *The Papers of Benjamin Franklin*. To the three learned and perceptive Franklinists who have worked so long and so skillfully as editors of *The Papers*—Leonard W. Labaree, Helen C. Boatfield, and Helene H. Fineman—I owe more than I can ever say. Conversations with David D. Hall and William H. Goetzmann of Yale University were most helpful at critical stages of the first draft. Whitfield J. Bell, Jr., of the American Philosophical Society and Stuart Gerry Brown of Syracuse University read and crit-

## *Preface*

icized the manuscript and in fact have long been my mentors in the Age of Franklin. Finally, the dedication records the inspiration for whatever insight I may have into Franklin's worth as a human being.

SYRACUSE UNIVERSITY                    R. L. K.
June 1964

# Chronology

1683    Franklin's father, Josiah, emigrates to New England.
1706    Born in Boston; baptized at Old South Church.
1722    "Silence Dogood" published in *New England Courant*.
1723    Runs away to Philadelphia.
1724-26 In England; works at printer's trade.
1725    Writes and prints *A Dissertation on Liberty and Necessity*.
1727    Forms the Junto.
1729    Begins publishing *The Pennsylvania Gazette*.
        Publishes pamphlet on paper currency.
1730    Appointed printer to the Pennsylvania Assembly. Takes Deborah Read to wife.
1731    Founds the Library Company of Philadelphia.
1732    Begins publishing *Poor Richard: An Almanack;* continued annually until 1758.
1735    Defends Rev. Samuel Hemphill.
1736    Appointed clerk of the Assembly. Forms Union Fire Company.
1737    Appointed postmaster of Philadelphia.
1739    Begins friendship with George Whitefield.
1741    Publishes *The General Magazine*.
1743    Publishes *Proposal for Promoting Useful Knowledge*.

1747   First writes of his electrical experiments. Writes *Plain Truth;* organizes first militia in Pennsylvania.

1748   Retires from active business.
Elected to the Philadelphia Common Council.

1749   Publishes *Proposals Relating to the Education of Youth in Pennsylvania;* active in founding the Academy of Philadelphia.

1751   His *Experiments and Observations on Electricity* first published in London.
Pennsylvania Hospital chartered.
Begins service in Pennsylvania Assembly; elected annually until 1764.
Writes *Observations Concerning the Increase of Mankind.*

1753   Receives honorary M.A. from Harvard and from Yale.
Appointed deputy postmaster general of North America.

1754   Proposes Albany Plan of Union; writes letters to Governor Shirley.

1755   Active aiding General Braddock, defending Pennsylvania against Indian attacks, and in writing antiproprietary messages for the Assembly.

1756   Elected Fellow of the Royal Society.
1757   Goes to England as Assembly agent.
Composes preface to *Poor Richard* for 1758, later known as "The Way to Wealth."

1759   Receives honorary LL.D. degree from University of St. Andrews.
Meets David Hume and Lord Kames.

1760   Writes *Interest of Great Britain Considered* (Canada pamphlet).
Secures Privy Council approval of taxation of proprietary estates in Pennsylvania.

1762   Receives honorary D.C.L. degree from Oxford University.
Returns to Philadelphia.

1764    Writes series of pamphlets on Pennsylvania politics.
        After a scurrilous campaign, defeated for re-election to the Assembly.
        Returns to England.
1765    Opposes Stamp Act and then works for its repeal; writes many anonymous pieces for the London press.
1766    Examined before the House of Commons on the Stamp Act.
1768    Writes *Causes of American Discontents Before 1768.*
        Appointed agent for Georgia.
1769    Elected president of the American Philosophical Society; re-elected annually during his life.
1770    Intense newspaper propaganda campaign against Townshend duties; repealed, except that on tea.
        Appointed agent for Massachusetts.
1771    Begins autobiography.
1772    Elected to French Academy of Sciences; one of eight foreign members.
1773    Writes famous satires attacking British imperial policy.
1774    Hears of Boston Tea Party; attacked before the Privy Council; dismissed as deputy postmaster general.
        Coercive acts passed; begins final negotiations with Lord Chatham and others to preserve the British Empire.
1775    Returns to America; elected to the Continental Congress and to the Pennsylvania Committee of Safety; active in support of war measures.
        Submits Articles of Confederation for United Colonies.
1776    Helps draft and signs Declaration of Independence.

|      | Presides at Pennsylvania Constitutional Convention. |
|------|-----------------------------------------------------|
|      | Sails for France as an American commissioner; has first audiences with French foreign minister Vergennes. |
| 1777 | Lionized by Parisian society and French intellectuals. |
|      | Obtains first subsidies (secret) from French government. |
| 1778 | Negotiates and signs French alliance. |
| 1779 | Receives appointment as minister to France. |
| 1780 | Harassed by onerous duties and plagued by quarrels with Arthur Lee and others, but retains and broadens French support of the American cause. |
| 1781 | Appointed a commissioner to negotiate peace; hears of American victory at Yorktown. |
| 1782 | With John Adams and John Jay, negotiates treaty of peace with Great Britain. |
|      | Writes *Information to Those Who Would Remove to America.* |
| 1783 | Fascinated by balloon ascensions in Paris. |
| 1784 | Negotiates treaties of commerce with Prussia and other European nations. |
|      | Resumes autobiography; writes *Remarks Concerning the Savages of North America.* |
| 1785 | Returns to Philadelphia. |
|      | Elected president of Pennsylvania; re-elected annually until 1788. |
| 1787 | Elected president of Pennsylvania Society for Promoting the Abolition of Slavery. |
|      | Delegate to the Federal Constitutional Convention. |
| 1789 | Finishes last long section of his autobiography. |
| 1790 | April 17: dies quietly at his home, aged 84 years, 3 months. |

# Chapter I

# Boyhood Training

WHAT FORMS THE mind of a bright and active boy? What results from an interplay of admonition, example, games, and books? When nearly seventy, Benjamin Franklin remembered that as a lad he had heard Increase Mather preach about the rumored death of "that wicked old Persecutor of God's People, Lewis XIV." Mather delivered the sermon on October 2, 1715, (Franklin was nine) amid warnings in Boston newspapers that the invasion of Scotland by Popish backers of the Stuart pretender to the British throne endangered the Protestant succession in England. The country had just finished over twenty years of exhausting warfare to prevent Louis XIV from extending absolutist and Catholic hegemony over western and central Europe. During the struggle, first called King William's and then Queen Anne's War in the colonies, Indians had ravaged the frontier from New England to the Carolinas. The wars were especially traumatic in Massachusetts. There savages assaulted peaceful villages and imperialist France threatened invasion. The treasonable attempt at home (as colonists called England) to supplant a cherished dynasty with a despised foreign one aroused the zeal of self-righteous Puritans, who saw the struggle for the Protestant succession as part of a crusade against diabolical Jesuits. Little wonder then that a nine-year-old boy found memorable a sermon by the lead-

ing minister of his city celebrating the death of
Louis XIV, the symbol of all he had been taught to
scorn and hate and fear.

The worldwide forces considered so important by
Increase Mather would have been made vivid to the
Franklins by the arrival in Boston at this time of
many Huguenot refugees driven from France by the
anti-Protestant edicts of Louis XIV. Among those
who arrived in 1715 was the father of Paul Revere.
Though the midnight ride and the Declaration of
Independence were sixty years in the future, already potentially revolutionary attitudes were forming in New England. Settlers there had long been
taught to honor the heroes of Cromwell's army who
had defied a king and defended the power of Parliament, and perhaps more than any other Britons
they had welcomed the "Glorious Revolution" of
1688, which had driven the last of the Stuart despots
from the English throne. They had long listened
as well to clergymen preach the need to seek and to
follow the dictates of conscience. The Franklins and
Reveres would have been aghast at the suggestion in
1715, but their fervent resistance to a French tyrant
in the name of conscience and of English constitutional liberty would be redirected when they felt oppressed by the British crown. The causes, excite-
ments, prejudices, and attitudes which occupied
the attention of Boston during Benjamin Franklin's
youth were full of meaning for the future of the
country and had a vast effect, of course, on the later
development of his mind.

Franklin told in his autobiography how as a boy
he "was generally a Leader," and in exploits on the
ponds and bays around Boston he "was commonly
allow'd to govern, especially in any case of Difficulty." On one occasion he led a group of youths who
took stones from a building site to construct a
fishing wharf on the mill pond. Franklin thought

this showed "an early projecting public Spirit, tho' not then justly conducted," and observed that "several of us were corrected by our Fathers; and, tho' I pleaded the Usefulness of the Work, mine convinc'd me that nothing was useful which was not honest." Evidently Franklin very early had a way of judging actions by their utility, a habit of taking the lead in projects, and an instinct for making dreams come true. The opportunity to live such a boyhood must have had an incalculable effect on the life of a man regarded for nearly half a century as Philadelphia's most useful citizen. The parental intervention, typical probably of the wise, firm guidance Josiah Franklin gave his seventeen children, must also have had a great effect in molding Franklin's mind and character. How many times, even if not always observed, would a conviction that "nothing was useful which was not honest" help decide a course of action or an attitude in public affairs? Benjamin Franklin honored his mother and father—what did their piety and prudential good sense mean to him? Before he read the many books he later remembered as important to him, he had learned many of the most important lessons of life from his parents and his playmates.

This early fusion of deed and thought, common enough in childhood, is especially important in Franklin's case because, more than with most of the world's great thinkers, his was a life of action. Some intellectual giants seem to have lived most of their lives in the study or at the writing desk. Perry Miller disposed of Jonathan Edwards' "external biography," the events of his life, in twenty-four pages and devoted over three hundred pages to what was important in Edwards' case, the brilliant, probing ideas he set down on paper. Immanuel Kant led a life carefully regulated to nourish his mind: he studied before breakfast, wrote and lectured in the morning, conversed in the afternoon, and read in the evening, almost never moving from his home and university and taking no part in the public affairs of his day. Franklin, on the other hand, had only a few years' schooling, and at age ten went to work in his father's candle and soap-making shop. His first published essays, written when he was sixteen, were in emulation of his brother's literary friends and satirized the then fashionable social customs, politics, and morality. Thereafter cause after cause and project after project enlisted his facile pen. Virtually all of his writing arose from particular circumstances, served an immediate purpose, and had a deliberate intent. If we may judge from the abundant written remains, his thought and philosophy grew hand in hand with the full life he led. To expound and analyze his ideas apart from the events which called them forth would be to miss their essence and meaning.

Daniel Boorstin has observed that "no American invention has influenced the world so powerfully as the concept of knowledge which sprang from the American experience . . . a man's mind [in eighteenth-century America] was wholesome not when it possessed the most refined implements for dissecting and ordering all knowledge, but when it was most sensitive to the unpredicted whisperings of environment." In this sense Franklin was the most American of Americans. Thus, though Franklin's education, beyond what has been said of the imponderable effect of his childhood experiences, must be described in terms of the books he read and the ideas he might have gleaned from them, it is necessary to remember that as soon as he is old enough to act importantly his mental biography is interwoven inextricably with the events of his life in the unique environment of the new world. His ideas cannot be extracted and sorted out according to some analytical scheme without robbing them of meaning. In fact, a harmony of thought and action was the seminal feature of his mind.

Benjamin Franklin informed his son that "this obscure Family of ours was early in the Reformation, and continu'd Protestants thro' the Reign of Queen Mary [1553-58], when they were sometimes in Danger of Trouble on Account of their Zeal against Popery." A favorite family anecdote told how during times of persecution the forbidden English Bible was strapped beneath a stool which could be uprighted quickly if, during family devotions, one of the children posted at the door saw "an Officer of the Spiritual Court" approaching. Franklin's father, Josiah, maintained his nonconformity under Charles II, and removed to New England in 1683 when the King's officers persisted in disturbing his worship. In Boston Josiah Franklin occupied a house within twenty yards of Old South Church, soon took an important part in its affairs, and reared his children faithfully according to its precepts. Few persons born in the English colonies in the eighteenth century came from a firmer Puritan, dissenting tradition than Benjamin Franklin.

This meant, of course, that as a boy he read the Bible, learned the catechism, took part in family devotions, and listened to long sermons. The Bible has been used by many people for many purposes and those inclined to quote it have managed to find support for almost every imaginable view, but in Boston, early in the eighteenth century, children brought up in the orthodox Puritan way learned clear and unmistakable lessons from it. If anyone wondered what its doctrines were, the catechism and the famous *New England Primer* quickly set the matter straight. Benjamin Franklin almost certainly received instruction from a simple catechism for children by John Cotton, *Spiritual Milk for Boston Babes, in Either England: Drawn out of the breasts of both Testaments for their Souls nourishment* (c. 1641).

Beginning with the question "What hath God done for you?" and answer "God hath made me, He keepeth me, and He can save me," it carried its students clearly and easily through the Calvinist doctrine of the Puritans. It taught that man was "conceived in sin and born in iniquity," that therefore he had a "corrupt nature bent . . . only unto sin," and that "Sin is the Transgression of the Law." The child learned the Ten Commandments and what each required and forbade. The fifth commandment, for example, honor thy father and thy mother, meant to revere and obey "all our Superiors . . . in Family, School, Church, and commonwealth," and the eighth, thou shalt not steal, forbade men "to take away another man's goods without his leave: or to spend our own without benefit to ourselves or others," and required them "to get our goods honestly, to keep them safely, and to spend them thriftily." The youth next learned that the wages of sin were death and damnation, that the only salvation was through Jesus Christ, and that the Law taught man his sin and God's wrath, thus making man feel his need for a redeeming grace. He learned finally that the church is a "Congregation of Saints joyned together in the bond of the Covenant to worship the Lord, and to edifie one another in all his holy Ordinances," and that at the last judgment "the Righteous shall go into life eternal, and the wicked shall be cast into everlasting fire with the Devil and his angels."

If perchance a youngster missed some of the lessons of Cotton's catechism, he was exposed to them again in the revered and ubiquitous Westminster catechism, first published in 1649. Following the famous doctrines that "Man's chief End is to Glorify God, and to Enjoy Him for ever" and that "the Word of God which is contained in the Scriptures of the old and new Testaments, is the only Rule to direct us how we may glorify and enjoy Him," the student learned that the benefits of salvation were "assurance of God's love, peace of conscience, joy in the Holy Ghost, increase of Grace, and perseverance therein to the end," and that "the Spirit of God maketh the Reading, but especially the Preaching of the Word an effectual Means of convincing and Converting Sinners, and of building them up in Holiness and Comfort, through Faith unto Salvation." In both catechisms abundant scriptural citations and quotations accompanied the answers and left no doubt that the Bible was the great authority on all the important questions of life and death. Cotton Mather, the leading Boston minister during Franklin's boyhood, admonished parents that "well catechized children, will be your Comfort, your Honour. . . . Your children will never be full of Goodness, if they are not filled with Knowledge . . . it is of Extreme Importance . . . that the *Understandings* of the children, should have the truths of the Gospel in them, as well as their *Memories.*"

Franklin's brief formal schooling (six months at about age eight) was probably sufficient to expose him to the moral and religious lessons imbedded in learning the ABC's. *The New England Primer* taught that "In *A*dam's fall, we sinned all," that "a *D*og will bite, a thief at night," that *"J*ob feels the rod, yet blesses God," and that *"W*hales in the sea, God's voice obey." The student was further instructed to "Learn these four Lines by Heart— Have Communion with few. Be Intimate with ONE. Deal justly with all. Speak Evil of none." He also memorized the graphic poetic exhortation of the martyred John Rogers, who advised children, among other things, to

> abhor the arrant whore of Rome
> and all her Blasphemies,
> and drink not of her cursed cup
> obey not her decrees . . .

Give of your Portion to the Poor
as Riches do arise;
and from the needy naked Soul
turn not away your eyes.

The catechizing and constant confrontation with
religious doctrine failed in its major purpose as far
as Franklin was concerned. When "scarce fifteen,"
he had rejected the faith and theology of his Puritan
forebears, but their moral outlook and earnest attitude toward life were too deeply implanted for
him ever to lose. When he learned of his mother's
grief over his heretical opinions, Franklin responded
that he thought "vital Religion had always suffer'd,
when orthodoxy is more regarded than Virtue. And
the Scripture assures me, that at the last Day, we
shall not be examin'd what we *thought*, but what
we *did;* and our Recommendation will not be that
we said *Lord, Lord*, but that we did GOOD to our
fellow Creatures." Franklin gradually developed
rational and utilitarian modes of thought to but-
tress his outlook on life, but its foundation was always in the habits and precepts of the faith in
which he had been reared.

# Chapter II

# Early Reading

FRANKLIN TELLS US that "from a Child I was fond of Reading, and all the little Money that came into my Hands was ever laid out in Books." As with many New Englanders, the book which stood first in his memory of boyhood reading was John Bunyan's *Pilgrim's Progress*. Delighted with it, he bought as his first collection "Bunyan's Works in separate little Volumes." He read the "Books in polemic Divinity" which filled his father's "little Library," but regretted the time spent on them. He devoured Plutarch's *Lives* ("time spent to great Advantage"), and bought forty or fifty volumes of Burton's historical collections, little books which melted English history down into anecdotes, curiosities, patriotism, moral lessons, and dramatic incidents. At about the same time he read Daniel Defoe's *Essay on Projects* and Cotton Mather's *Essays to do Good*. With this reading, done while the incessant religious instruction continued, Franklin began the transformation of doctrine into precepts, of sermons into good works, which remained the special mark of his genius as long as he lived. These books reinforced the habits learned in his daily round of boyhood life.

In retrospect one finds it difficult to reconstruct anything of the impact of Bunyan's *Pilgrim's Progress* in the New England of Franklin's youth, where it ranked with the Bible and a few psalters,

primers, and catechisms as a "best seller." One suspects, though, that its moral earnestness, presented
in the vivid, poignant metaphors of the best Puritan
writing, was what impressed the young Franklin.
The impression was doubtless the stronger because
Bunyan had lived and preached in Bedford, England,
only a few miles from the Franklin ancestral home
in Ecton. Josiah Franklin moved to New England
five years after publication of *Pilgrim's Progress*.
If he had not heard Bunyan preach, stories of the
zealous minister imprisoned for his faith must have
been known and revered among the dissenting
Franklins.

Benjamin Franklin probably applauded Bunyan's
apology for the mode adopted to tell the story of a
truly Christian life:

Solidity, indeed, becomes the pen
Of him that writeth things divine to men:
But must I needs want solidness, because
By metaphors I speak? Were not God's laws,
His gospel laws, in older times held forth
By shadows, types, and metaphors?

As for the book's purpose:

Yea it will make the slothful active be;
The blind also delightful things to see . . .
. . . read my fancies; they will stick like burrs,
And may be to the helpless comforters.

Bunyan proposed to display the essential Christian
qualities and the way they guided conduct by telling
an allegory of the journey through life of his hero,
Christian, as he went from the vale of woe called
earth to the bliss of Heaven.

As Christian struggles along the difficult pilgrimage to the Celestial City, his character and that
of those he meets along the way emerge vividly. In
the very first incident, as Christian leaves the City

of Destruction, he deals with two clear human types:
Obstinate, who refuses to see any of Christian's
vision and ridicules his pilgrimage, and Pliable, who,
pulled both ways, decides to go with Christian, is
disheartened by the difficulties of the Slough of
Despond, and finally, turning back, takes the easy
way out. Whatever one might think of Bunyan's
theology, the lessons for everyday life are unmistakable. The person of perseverance and faith pro-
gresses while the stubborn skeptic and fainthearted
doubter are left to the sure fruits of their own
folly and lack of fortitude. Some characters along
the way—Mr. Worldly-wiseman (a liar), Mr. Le-
gality (a cheat) and his son Mr. Civility (a hypo-
crite), the Man of Despair, Simple, Sloth, Presumption, Ignorance, Formalist and Hypocrisy, Ti-
morous and Mistrust, Talkative and Mr Say-well
(empty professors)—personify traits to be shunned.
Others—Help, Piety, Prudence, Charity, Faithful,
and Hopeful—display the qualities which lead along
the path of righteousness. Of the places along the
way, some—Carnal Policy, the Valley of Humilia-
tion, and Vanity Fair (where Christian met Beel-
zebub and his friends Lord Luxurious, Lord Lechery,
and Sir Having Greedy)—were fraught with danger to the pilgrim, while others, such as the House
called Beautiful and the Delectable Mountains, offered succor and support. The journey of Christian's
family, though less perilous, dramatizes anew the
qualities which bless or doom life.

Like fabulists and storytellers of every age, Bunyan set the faith and wisdom of his day down in
indelible terms. Though Franklin secularized the
pilgrimage in his own life, the qualities he admired
were those Bunyan extolled, and those he warned
against were those Bunyan shunned. Franklin's autobiography tells of a journey to an earthly city,
but the way he recommends for pilgrims is one
best traveled by those who have learned the lessons
of Christian's quest of the Celestial City. Even had

Franklin not told us that *Pilgrim's Progress* impressed him, we might have guessed it, for the life he lived and the story he told about it bear unmistakably the stamp of that early reading in his father's "little Library."

The other works of Bunyan which Franklin bought with the first money he saved for books tell the same story all over again. In *A Discourse upon the Pharisee and the Publican* (reprinted in London in 1705 in an octavo volume Franklin might have purchased), Bunyan used the parable Franklin probably knew by heart to emphasize some important lessons. He admonished the pharisee who thanked God he was not like the publican: "Modesty should have commanded thee to have bit thy tongue as to this . . . thou shouldest have remembered this thy Brother in this his Day of adversity, and shouldest have shewed, that thou hadst Compassion to thy Brother in this his deplorable Condition." Other works, such as his autobiography *(Grace abounding to the Chief of Sinners); The Life and Death of Mr. Badman; The Barren Fig Tree, or the Doom and Downfall of the Fruitless Professor; Instruction for the Ignorant, an Easy Dialogue;* and *A Book for Boys and Girls,* proclaim over and over again in vivid, simple language that if man is wicked, selfish, and slothful, he is doomed, but if he is diligent, benevolent, repentant, and faithful, he may find glory. This serious attitude toward life, never for a moment doubting that its purpose is real and earnest, is Franklin's chief legacy from his Puritan forebears. It is significant that he took for his chief teacher their greatest storyteller and dramatist of life's battles. Like the faithful minister of Bedford, the printer of Philadelphia understood theology best when it was embodied in the conduct of life, and knew that a purposeful striving was the only salvation for man. Bunyan sent a shaft directly at Franklin's heart when he turned religious doctrine into a way of life.

When Josiah Franklin took his youngest son out
of Boston Grammar School to work in the family
chandlery, he barred the boy from the thorough
soaking in Greek and Latin undergone by nearly all
learned men of the day, but at the same time he may
have saved him from the sterile scholasticism such
training inflicted on many minds. As an early critic
of Franklin's writings put it, if he had had a formal
education, his "powerful understandings [might]
have been lost in the Dialectics of Aristotle . . . he
[might] have contented himself with expounding the
metres of Pindar." Indeed, the unpretentious creativ-
ity of Franklin's mind as well as his later disdain
for the ancient languages may be traceable to the
early impressment into the family business. But even
as a youth he was not entirely ignorant of the heritage of Greece and Rome, which, together with Christian teachings, was the bedrock of seventeenth- and
eighteenth-century learning. He was lucky indeed,
if we may assume he had an early interest in the
qualities which make men truly great, to find the
volumes of Plutarch's *Lives* in his father's library.
He probably read them in English translation, perhaps that done in 1579 by Sir Thomas North using
the vigorous idiom familiar to us in Shakespeare and
in the King James and Douay versions of the Bible.
From Plutarch Franklin learned of the classical
concern for the public character of men and for
the commonweal. While the catechisms and the works
of Bunyan led youths to care for the salvation of
their individual souls, Plutarch, following Plato,
taught them the importance of being wise and good
citizens.

His mixture of moral precept and practical advice
for promoting social harmony find echo after echo
in Franklin's later career. For example, Plutarch
praised Publicola, the founder of the Roman republic, because he "took great heed not only to get his
goods more justly but those which he had, he spent
most honestly in helping the needy." Plutarch fur-

ther observed that "a wise governor of a realm and politic man doth govern diversely according to the occasions offered, taking everything in his time wherein he will deal. And many times in letting go one thing, he saveth the whole, and in losing a little he gaineth much." It is seldom possible to say what parts of a book will stick in the mind of a reader, but it seems fair to guess that Franklin, noticing the men of Boston coming to his father's house to discuss church and town affairs, would have paid particular attention to such precepts as these, brought to life in the deeds of Plutarch's characters. In recounting the life of Pericles, Plutarch scolded those who learn things vain and unprofitable "and who neglect things honest and necessary to be learned," and advised his readers to be like Pericles and his Roman "parallel," Fabius Maximus, "marvelous profitable members for their country." He praised Pericles for the wonderful buildings and statues he had erected in Athens and noted his special skill in governing a city "puffed up with pride and presumption of long prosperity," a more difficult task than that of Fabius who, during Hannibal's invasion of Italy, ruled "a city already brought low by adversity and which, compelled by necessity, is contented to be governed by a wise man."

In a passage which must have pleased Josiah Franklin as he sought to teach his son the importance of being a *good man*, Plutarch began his comparison of Alexander the Great and Julius Caesar by declaring that "my intent is not to write history, but only lives. For the noblest deeds do not always show men's virtues and vices, but oftentimes a light occasion, a word, or some sport makes men's natural dispositions and manners appear more plain than the famous battles of war wherein are slain ten thousand men." The account of Alexander is full of stories showing his courage, magnanimity, skill in leading men, and respect for learning. Plutarch told with admiration of Caesar's reproof when his companions complained of some simple food served them by a friend: "it had been enough . . . to have abstained to eat of what they disliked, and not to shame their friend." Franklin, the youthful wharf-builder, must have marveled at Caesar's great feat of building a bridge across the swift and treacherous Rhine. Plutarch made clear, though, the legacy of Caesar's lust for power: "he reaped no other fruit of his reign and dominion which he had so vehemently desired all his life, and pursued with such extreme danger, but a vain name only, and a superficial glory that procured him the envy and hatred of his country."

In noting the humble origins of Demosthenes and Cicero, Plutarch stated another precept dear to Josiah Franklin's heart and always honored by his son: "if we chance to offend and live not as we should, we cannot accuse the meanness of our country where we were born, but we must justly accuse ourselves." Benjamin Franklin must have admired Demosthenes for his diligence in practicing oratory month after month in a cellar, for learning to speak with pebbles in his mouth to cure his stuttering, and for shouting while running uphill to give force to his naturally "small and soft voice." By such intrepid effort are self-made men fashioned. Plutarch admonished Cicero for his vanity, which often "made him swerve from justice," but praised him because he "of all men in Rome, made the Romans know how much eloquence doth grace and beautify that which is honest, and how invincible right and justice are, being eloquently set forth." Unforgivably, though, Cicero acquiesced in Caesar's dictatorship, "a more grievous and greater tyranny" than that of Catiline, which Cicero had led in suppressing.

In reading these sharply drawn character sketches, Franklin learned not only that a man's moral standing marked his real worth, but also that no man could be self-respecting unless he devoted himself steadfastly and actively to the welfare of his country. When Franklin, in the midst of bitter political strife, told a friend that "I am not much concern'd . . . if I have offended [the Proprietors] *by acting right,* [because] I can, whenever I please, remove their displeasure *by acting wrong,* tho' at present I have not the least Inclination to be in their good Graces on those Terms," he spoke as Plutarch over and over again had had his heroes speak. When he wrote of his disgust at "the extream corruption prevalent among all Orders of Men in this old rotten State [England], and the glorious publick Virtue so predominant in our rising Country, I cannot but apprehend more Mischief than Benefit from a closer Union," and then at age seventy signed the Declaration of Independence and departed on a perilous voyage to France to seek aid for the new nation, he acted as a Plutarchian hero. No praise could have pleased Franklin more than that accorded him when, before the French Academy, he was compared to Solon, whom Plutarch had extolled as the great lawgiver of antiquity.

In the last analysis, Christianity teaches man to put the care of his soul, his conscience, and his obedience to the will of God above his obligations as a citizen of the earthly city. Thus it limits in a fundamental way man's public responsibilities, and commands him to disobey man-made law if it conflicts with conscience. It teaches him a certain detachment from the affairs of mere men. As a Puritan, Franklin had been taught an extreme version of this primary commitment to conscience and God's will. Plutarch's stories of the noble Greeks and Romans, judged by their patriotism as well as by their personal qualities, may have served as an important counterpoise to the preoccupation with his own soul which Franklin learned from his parents and other spiritual preceptors.

Had Franklin remained a businessman and mor-

alist and not undertaken when past forty his long
career as a politician and diplomat, his early education in the principles of public life would require
little comment. Had he written more about the
axioms and propositions *basic* to his public career,
we might be justified in paying little attention to
his boyhood exposures. As it is, though, they are
of the utmost importance as a source of fundamentals and because Franklin's life was so much a
public one. He could have had no more propitious an
introduction to the ideals of service to one's country
than that afforded by Plutarch's *Lives*. His guiding
principles are reverence for constitutional forms and
government by law, a conviction that defense of
the public welfare depends on the courage and
virtue of those entrusted with office, a belief that
heroic, steadfast conduct is what makes great men,
and that such men do indeed direct the course of
human affairs. These ideals made an indelible impression on Franklin and are visible behind his activities as a public servant before and after he left
Philadelphia in 1757, and before and after the
Declaration of Independence. If a schooling in the
axioms of public service is deemed practical and
desirable, and if Franklin is admired for his service,
then Plutarch deserves the first rank as a preceptor.
He taught Franklin to fulfill diligently his dual
citizenship roles, to rule and be ruled with honor
and responsibility.

When Franklin read Richard Burton's little history, travel, adventure, and conduct books. he found
the romance and wonders which excited the English-
speaking world of his day told according to its taste.
Burton, actually the printer Nathaniel Crouch
(1632?-1725?), wrote a series of very popular,
cheap (one shilling each) "pocket books," frequently revised and reissued, which mix and combine
the qualities of Richard Halliburton's *Book of
Marvels*, *The Reader's Digest*, *Boy's Life*, and

Parson Weems's *Life of George Washington*. In today's book trade, his volumes would have sold by the millions at drugstores across the land, and other millions of copies would have been distributed by book clubs and supermarkets. Through him the unsophisticated public learned its history, its patriotism, its geography, and its manners. One title, an eighteenth-century equivalent of the lurid cover or dust jacket, may suggest why a New England boy, tired of sermons and catechisms, would have saved his pennies to buy the books: *Unparallel'd varieties: or, The matchless actions and passions of Mankind. Displayed in near four hundred notable instances and examples. Discovering the transcendent effects: I. Of love, friendship, and gratitude. II. Of magnanimity, courage, and fidelity. III. Of charity, temperance, and humility. And on the contrary, the tremendous consequences. IV. Of hatred, revenge, and ingratitude. V. Of cowardice, barbarity, and treachery. VI. Of unchastity, intemperance, & ambition. Imbellished with pictures.*

Drama, excitement, and marvels fill every page. In *The History of the Nine Worthies of the World*, deeds of courage and daring are featured, and the heroes do indeed make history. All nine worthies were great soldiers: three gentiles, Hector of Troy, Alexander the Great, and Julius Caesar (the last two accounts taken from Plutarch); three Jews, Joshua, David, and Judas Maccabeus; and three Christians, King Arthur, Charlemagne, and King Godfrey of Jerusalem. A companion piece, *Female Excellency, or the Ladies Glory, Illustrated in the Lives and memorable Actions of Nine Famous Women . . . the whole adorned with Poems and the Picture of each Lady*, pointed out the virtues admirable in the fairer sex as seen in the lives of "Valiant Judith," "the chast Lucretia," Clotilda, Queen of France, and others. In a book about the monarchs of England, Burton detailed the fifteen ways William the Conqueror had oppressed the people of England

and observed that "he was feared by many, but loved by few," though he was praised as of "undaunted Courage, resolute in Action, and quick in Execution." Henry II is admired for his wise administration and for his conquests in France and Ireland, but is condemned for keeping a mistress and for the murder of Thomas à Becket. Burton told graphically of Henry's passion and lust for his concubine, of her murder by the Queen, and of the bloody scene at Canterbury when Henry's assassins slew Becket. One can imagine a boy thirsting for adventure utterly enthralled. The other rulers also appear vividly. Queen Mary, for example, is held up as a bloody persecutor. During her reign, by Burton's accounting, 277 martyrs were hung or burned, including twenty-six wives, twenty widows, nine virgins, two boys, and two infants, "one sprung out of his Mother's Womb as she was burning at the Stake, and most unmercifully flung into the Fire at the very birth." Furthermore, "seven were whipt . . . [and] twelve buried in Dunghills."

*The Life and Dangerous Voyages of Sir Francis Drake* offered a wide scope for Burton's imagination and narrative gifts. The strange customs of the Indians, the cruelty of the Spanish, and the perils of the sea are the staples of the journal of Drake's voyage around the world. In the account of the battle with the Spanish Armada (1588) his heroic qualities become legendary: the crippled Spanish galleon (a floating castle) of the famous Don Pedro Valdez commanded to surrender at first refused, but upon learning Drake had made the demand, "instantly yielded . . . protesting they would have died, before they yielded to any save him, whom MARS and NEPTUNE always attended, and whose Civility to the Conquered had often been experienced." The English Civil War (1642-49) furnished Burton with endless tales of warfare, gore, and valor. The growth and success of Cromwell's army is told in detail, and though his military dictatorship is deplored, his "singular courage . . . and greatness of mind" are praised. In a history of *The Wars in England, Scotland, and Ireland,* published during the reign of Charles II, however, Puritan excesses are condemned, and the unjust trial and execution of Charles I (a "horrid and nefarious act") is described with a sense of drama Perry Mason would envy.

*A History of the House of Orange,* published in 1693, best illustrates Burton's historical method. He was led to tell of King William III's glorious ancestors "because we have such a furious Generation of Murmurers, who if they had their desires would ruine both themselves and their Countrey, and reduce us to French Popery and Slavery . . . both our Eternal and Temporal happiness very much depends upon the supporting the present Government against all its Foreign and Domestick Enemies. A Government founded upon Law and Justice; A Government calculated for the support of the Protestant Interest throughout the World." Next come accounts of the Dutch battle for independence from Spain, William of Orange's struggle with Louis XIV, and his accession to the English throne, thus deposing the Catholic James II. This history formed the epic backdrop for English patrotism during the eighteenth century, a patriotism Franklin shared fervently until he was sixty or more years old.

Harking back to the earliest days of the Reformation and glorying in England's deliverance from the Spanish Armada, Britons of the eighteenth century saw the so-called second hundred years' war with France, begun in 1689, as a renewal of the fight for national and religious independence. Burton's histories reinforced Franklin's inherited Puritan belief that every ounce of energy and every patriotic feeling must be directed against the Pope and the King of France, who were in league to enslave England and her colonies. This mingling of

national and religious commitment, so foreign to
Americans after nearly two hundred years' devotion to separation of church and state, and which
seems today so intolerant and bigoted, was in fact
for the young Franklin the equivalent of the belief
in a free society taught in our schools or, to use
a less analogous example, of the Communist ideology
and love of "Mother Russia" taught young people
in the Soviet Union.

Burton's travel books, telling of newly discovered
lands populated with strange people and fantastic
animals, must have left youthful readers in wide-
eyed amazement. Marriage and burial customs nearly always receive special attention. Strange and
heretical religions suffer by comparison with enlightened Christianity. The Mohammedans are
marked out invariably as objects of horror and fear,
as though Burton sought to rekindle the passions of
the Crusades. The riches to be won in the New
World are held out to dazzle the reader:

Nay in this Bounteous and this Blessed Land,
The Golden Ore lies mixt with Common Sand.

To make his stories more real, Burton often copied
long extracts from travelers' accounts. For example,
in *Extraordinary Adventures, Revolutions and
Events, Being an account of Divers Stupendious
Accidents, Strange Deliverances, Signal Mutations
in the Fortunes of Several Famous Men, and Changes
of Government in Many Countries,* he reprinted
twenty pages of the journal of an Englishman captured by the Barbary pirates, telling of strange
beasts, wild lands, and concluding with "the several
ways of Execution" he had observed. If such reading was Franklin's first acquaintance with the peoples and customs of other lands, he must have seen
the world, like many people during the age of discovery, as a place full of adventure and challenge
and novelty.

As an alert publisher, Burton doubtless guessed
that readers enthralled by his histories and travel
stories would buy and perhaps profit from some
more explicit moralizing. He prepared the way by
telling of *The Unfortunate Court Favorites of
England,* unhappy people such as Elizabeth's Essex
and Charles I's Strafford who compromised their
integrity to flatter their masters and afterward received their just rewards from the public execu-
tioner. In the introduction to *The Unhappy Prin-
cesses,* the stories of Anne Boleyn and Lady Jane
Grey, readers were told that "Both the stories are
very Instructive and Serious, and possibly some
young Persons may be inclin'd to read them, rather
than the Productions of those vain and Frothy
Wits, who fill the World with Senseless, Atheistical
and Ridiculous Amusements, which tend only to
corrupt the Mind." In *The Young Man's Calling, or
The Whole Duty of Youth . . . together with Remarks upon the Lives of Several Excellent Young
Persons of both Sexes,* Burton gave the standard
advice of parents, preachers, and moral preceptors:
be good, be obedient, be pious, be diligent, be honest,
etc., illustrated in the lives of Isaac, Joseph, and
several princes of England. Though by itself this
could scarcely have seemed notable to a boy of
Franklin's careful rearing, it may have had some
force coming from the author who seemed to have
in his hands the keys to the wonders of the world,
just as moral homilies from an astronaut impress
young people in a way mere teachers or parents
never can.

The ideas important in forming the minds of
men who themselves later make contributions to
intellectual history are too seldom sought in the
popular wisdom, the events and causes dominant
during their youth. This wisdom, by its very com-
monness and by its almost inevitable overthrow by
new ideas already at work on more sophisticated

levels of society, has a way of being ignored by historians, who are themselves more interested in the forward edge of the human mind than in its broader, less penetrating part. Furthermore, the events and causes appear to us as history has come to judge them, not as they seemed to contemporaries. Thus in looking at "the mind" of the late seventeenth and early eighteenth century, students today see Newton, Hobbes, Locke, and Leibniz as the leading figures, but it is doubtful that Franklin read any of them before he was fifteen, and it was too early for very much popularized writing to show signs of their influence. Though Franklin's intellectual "conversion" to the new ideas was complete and vastly important in the development of his mind, the residue left in it by youthful reading of Bunyan, Plutarch, and Burton was very great indeed. The problem, as we observe Franklin reading the new books and formulating his own philosophy of life, is to understand the *mixture;* he did not read Wollaston on religion or Shaftesbury's ethics with a blank mind. He read them with a mind well furnished with the orthodoxies, prejudices, and wisdom of his childhood rearing and reading.

Consider as well how Franklin's view of the world from Boston in, say, 1715, when he heard Increase Mather rejoice in Louis XIV's death, differs from that which we receive of that same world in our history books. Our conventional wisdom sees English history, for example, as a growth of constitutional government and parliamentary power during the reigns of the Stuart and Hanoverian monarchs. We deplore those who seem to us to be fanatics or military despots. Thus Cromwell and even the Duke of Marlborough as well as Charles I and James II appear as obstacles to the steady progress of parliamentary supremacy. In 1715, though, feelings in Puritan New England permitted no such balanced view. The prospect of a tyrannical Stuart overthrow of the Protestant monarchy in England and the threat of a French-Catholic domination of Europe and its New World dependencies were all too real. If beheading a king or slaughtering Catholic rebels in Ireland or starving French peasants would help The Cause, that was a small price to pay in a desperate struggle for survival. That the rhetoric of the battle was at heart as much religious as national or dynastic did not seem to men on either side unusual or intolerant; it simply recognized the fact that in the seventeenth and early eighteenth centuries as a matter of course religions depended on force of arms for support and nations used religious passions to bolster morale at home and on the battlefield. Richard Burton's histories reflected this world view and are more relevant in understanding Franklin's outlook, of course, than the writings of Macaulay or Churchill, which color our knowledge of English history.

It is difficult, too, for us to grasp the excitement and fantasy which accompanied the discovery and exploration by Europeans of the three-quarters or more of the globe virtually unknown to them before the sixteenth century. This included the new, almost unsettled lands of Africa and the New World as well as the rich, ancient civilizations of the Orient. One suspects that the wonders of space of our own day, even in science fiction, probably do not have the electrifying qualities and certainly are less real for us than stories of Timbuktu, the Spanish Main, and Cathay were to an imaginative boy in Boston in 1715. Franklin testified to his intoxication with these marvels when he recorded that "I was very fond of voyages"; that is, of the fabulous stories of exploration told in such collections as Richard Hakluyt's *The Principall Navigations, Voiages, and Discoveries of the English Nation.* Franklin learned not only that the way of life in which he had been reared had its roots in books as old as the Bible and Plutarch's *Lives,* but that the world in which he lived was boundless in extent and opportunities, that the nation of which he was a part had assumed the leading role in founding new plantations, and that *he* lived in a part of the new empire having perhaps the most dazzling prospects of all. It is not surprising that the world view he acquired was expansive and full of great hopes and aspirations.

Like every appeal on behalf of national greatness, Burton's involved compromises which in some measure infected Franklin's zealous patriotism. In extending England's influence around the world, what of the natives who stood in the way? The tales of discovery which were the best sellers of Franklin's day did not boggle at the aggressions of explorers and conquistadors. The bloody deeds of Drake on the Spanish Main or Cromwell in Ireland were described with a pride untempered by regret for their cruelty. Burton never doubted, as Franklin never did, that human freedom and progress were tied inextricably to the supremacy of Protestant power in the world. Since England was a principal bulwark of that power, Englishmen who took pride in their country felt themselves at the same time upholding the cause of liberty itself. Franklin's recollection of Burton should remind us that before he was an advocate of independence according to natural law and a philosopher at home in any land of liberty, he had been British to the core and he believed fervently in all the shibboleths of her pursuit of national greatness.

As Franklin grew, he seems to have turned naturally from such boyhood exploits as wharf-building to a more responsible interest in community welfare. He was fortunate in this transition to come upon Daniel Defoe's *Essay upon Projects* (London, 1695), a book which combined a bourgeois spirit of enterprise with an almost saintly concern for the good of all mankind. As the title suggests, it contains proposals, or projects, for contending with a

host of social problems. The spirit and method are
consistent throughout: a description of an evil
couched to make the need for redress perfectly obvious; an assumption that reason and common sense
can yield a solution; a proposal for laws, associations, or cooperative effort as a means of solution;
detailed, practical suggestions for carrying out the
proposal; and a rebuttal of objections which might
be brought against the plan. Defoe thus proposes
plans to reform banks, repair the roads, provide
pensions for the aged, direct the gambling instinct
toward socially useful ends, care for lunatics, elim-
inate the iniquities of the bankruptcy laws, establish
an institute of good English usage, found a national military academy and schools for women,
prevent the abuses of impressing seamen on war-
ships, and insure houses against fire, individuals
against accidents, and widows against poverty.

One is struck over and over with how much Defoe's book foreshadows the attitude and method of
Franklin's career as a civic leader. Observing that
"Man is the worst of all God's creatures to shift
for himself," Defoe proposes that projectors really
deserving of that name must eschew mere money-
making schemes, which often cheat the public, but
must instead, like Noah building the ark, lay plans
to serve mankind. He praises the Romans, "the
Pattern of the whole World for Improvement and
Increase of arts and Learning, Civilizing and Meth-
odizing Nations," for their wonderful roads, which
after fifteen centuries were still a blessing to the
people of England. He then proposes laws to organize
the kingdom from Parliament down to every parish
to make England's roads her glory instead of her
shame. Defoe's plan that people make small contributions throughout life to care for their old age
foreshadows modern social-security plans. He outlined a careful scheme of association and payment
to build up a pension fund. What man, Defoe asked,
cannot afford "the expence of *Two Pots of Beer a*

*Month"* to provide security for his old age? He
finds the sport made of those born without reason
(fools) scandalous, and proposes that those born
with an abundance of reason (authors) pay a tax
on the sale of their books to support an asylum for
the fools.

The bankrupt is the particular object of Defoe's
compassion. How, he asks, can their imprisonment
be accounted just to them or beneficial to their creditors? Though Defoe wants rigorous laws against
fraudulent declarations of bankruptcy and grasping
creditors who seek revenge more than payment,
he proposes mild, reasonable procedures to permit
honest men to work to pay deserving creditors. The
logic is simple: if men owe, they must be able to
work if they are ever to pay—a proposition, Defoe
thought, any creditor of sense and charity must understand. In proposing an academy for women, Defoe
remarks that "one of the most barbarous customs in
the world . . . [is denying] the advantages of Learning to Women." Why think women are mentally inferior when they are taught only "to Stitch and
Sow, or make Bawbles? . . . What is a Man good for,
that is taught no more? . . . I cannot think God
Almighty ever made [women] so delicate, so glorious Creatures, and furnish'd them with such Charms,
so Agreeable and so Delightful to Mankind, with
Souls capable of the same accomplishments with
Men, and all to be only Stewards of our Houses,
*Cooks and Slaves. . . . I wou'd have Men take Women
for Companions, and Educate them to be fit for it."*

*Essay upon Projects* is, in short, a testament of
goodwill toward men and a handbook for giving
effect to that goodwill. It is a monument in words
to the spirit of the early, empirical, English Enlightenment, full of enthusiasm for and optimistic about
applying reason to improve human life, but still di-
recting its concern toward immediate, pressing problems rather than indulging the passion of the later,
continental Enlightenment for abstractions and pan-

aceas. This attitude and concern was the dominant
theme of Benjamin Franklin's life. It permeated all
his civic promotions, lurked behind his interest in
science, and presided over his politics and diplomacy.
More than any other person, Franklin brought into
being projects proposed by Defoe or projects true
to his spirit. Though Defoe's practical civic-minded-
ness had little influence in Augustan England (he is
remembered now principally as the author of *Rob-
inson Crusoe)*, his words found receptive eyes in
Franklin's and fell upon fertile ground in eighteenth-
century Philadelphia. Franklin never wrote a treatise on society, its ills, and their cure. It is doubtful
that he had a systematic social theory from which
he derived his dozens of promotions for social improvement. In the spirit of Defoe he encountered
problems one at a time, considered them with benevolence, and applied himself earnestly to their solution. Such an approach, of course, hardly seems
startling in a new land where a dearth of forms and
traditions invites ingenious proposals to deal with
a host of unforeseen circumstances. It is nevertheless
likely that Defoe's book gave one creative mind a
crucial impulse down a road doubtless wider and
more open in America than in the Old World.

Defoe also provided an important span in the
bridge from piety to secularism one crosses in moving from John Bunyan to Franklin. Brought up
in the same dissenting tradition as Franklin, Defoe
was in some ways Franklin's English counterpart.
In projecting Protestant earnestness, enterprise,
and individualism into the worlds of commerce and
public affairs, Defoe taught Franklin that goodwill,
reason, diligence, and ingenuity were the great tools
with which to build a better society. Though Bunyan would have abhorred the secularism of Defoe
and Franklin just as they discarded his theology, the
connections among the three men are significant
and unmistakable. Together they bespeak a mainstream of thought immensely important to western

civilization. They made the unflagging energy and zeal to improve the world inherent in their religious tradition readily available to men in all walks of life. With the effective translation of this spirit into habits of life and institutions for social progress, the modern world as we know it received its characteristic mark.

When Franklin promoted his first scheme for individual and civic welfare, the Junto of young tradesmen he organized in Philadelphia in 1727, he probably had Defoe's *Projects* in mind, but he turned specifically to proposals found in Cotton Mather's *Essays to do Good* (Boston, 1710). After reminding his readers that those who do good often must endure the misunderstanding, ingratitude, and envy of their neighbors, Mather expounds at length the religious reasons for doing good and then, in the part which inspired Franklin, proposes "Social Meetings for Religion" and "Associations of Young Men" to encourage habits of piety and altruism. Those who met for such purposes, wrote Mather, "have, like so many coals of the altar, kept one another alive, and been the means of maintaining a lively Christianity in the neighborhood." Among other things, the neighborhood societies "should consider themselves, as bound up in one bundle of love . . . If any one in the society should fall into affliction, all the rest should immediately study to relieve and support the afflicted person in every possible way. . . . They will, upon all just occasions, affectionately give and receive mutual admonitions on account of any thing which they may see amiss in each other." The men were counseled to "now and then spend half an hour . . . considering . . . *What good is there to be done?*" Who in adversity needed comfort? Who in contention needed a soothing word? Who in transgression needed admonition? They were told to "look out for some other hopeful young man . . . to engage him in the resolutions of godliness, until he also

shall be united to the society," and when the society
thus grew large, it should divide and spread its good
influence throughout the city.

Though Franklin secularized Mather's plan in organizing his Junto, the debt is nevertheless unmistakable. The Junto met regularly, worked diligently for the personal improvement of its members, pledged mutual aid, concerned itself with civic
welfare, and sought zealously to establish other jun-
tos. It seems perfectly clear that the Junto was the
heart and soul of Franklin's remarkable growth and
development during his young manhood in Philadelphia. In it, with good and close friends, he acquired self-discipline, formulated the maxims of
private and public conduct which guided the rest of
his life, and learned that men of goodwill working
together could indeed accomplish miracles. If Franklin had brought nothing from Boston to Philadelphia
but this secularized inspiration from *Essays to do
Good*, he would have had probably *the* essential
quality for making him Philadelphia's most valued
citizen during the last sixty years of his life. Mather,
the Puritan clergyman, gave to Franklin an earnest
sense of moral duty which, combined with Defoe's
buoyant optimism about applying reason to social
problems, produced a nearly ideal stimulus for effective action to alleviate human want and suffering.
One wonders if any civic leader ever had a better
training in a reflex action to do good than Benjamin
Franklin.

Many students of Franklin, fascinated with his
"conversion" to the secularism of the eighteenth
century, have slighted the habits and conceptions of
his childhood, an omission especially surprising in
twentieth-century writers, who, one would suppose,
would be keenly aware of Freudian doctrines of the
primary importance of early impressions and training. The contents of the books Franklin remembered
as important to him as a boy have been recounted

in some detail to emphasize the furnishings of mind which underwent the alleged conversion. He had a thorough indoctrination in the conventional wisdom of his day, equivalent to (though vastly different from, of course) the indoctrination one would get today from our best sellers, popular magazines, television programs, and handbooks of self-help and goodwill. We must remember again that the most important requisite in understanding Franklin's thought is to measure the mixture, conscious and otherwise, which took place in his mind as he read the new wisdom and adopted so much of it as his own.

# Chapter III

# Skepticism and Orthodoxy

From Franklin's account in his autobiography, it is clear that his introduction to sophisticated, skeptical writing came unabetted by his father, though one suspects Josiah Franklin was too wise, as Benjamin grew older, to try to censor his reading. The shift from parental to self-direction in learning, at any rate, came decisively at age twelve in 1718, when Benjamin was apprenticed to his brother James, in his second year as a Boston printer. In the printing shop, as Benjamin recalled later, "I had Access to better Books. . . . Often I sat up in my Room reading the greatest Part of the Night." Franklin reveled in his wonderful new world of words, soon began imitating the poets he read, and undertook to dispute with other youths the new doctrines he encountered. The most important book he discovered was "an odd Volume of the Spectator": he "bought it, read it over and over, and was much delighted with it." How Franklin tried to imitate its style by writing on the same subjects as *The Spectator,* comparing his efforts with the original, and then correcting by searching for better words or more concise sentences, is a well-known story. In this way he developed the clear, sharp expression which still makes him one of the most widely admired writers in English. Later he often remarked on the advantages acquired in business and in public life because, as he put it, "of my having learnt a little to scribble."

The measured elegance of Addison's prose, added to the vigor and directness of Bunyan and Defoe, gives Franklin's style its superb clarity and effectiveness. His own advice on style marks him unmistakably as heir to the English Enlightenment: good writing "ought to have a tendency to benefit the reader, by improving his virtue or his knowledge . . . it should proceed regularly from things known to things unknown, distinctly and clearly without confusion. The words used should be the most expressive that the language affords, provided they are the most generally understood. Nothing should be expressed in two words that can be as well expressed in one . . . the whole should be as short as possible, consistent with clearness. The words should be so placed as to be agreeable to the ear in reading; summarily, it should be *smooth, clear,* and *short."* Seldom have means and ends been so harmonious as they became when Franklin developed this *way* of writing to set down the sentiments he came to hold as he absorbed the new learning of his day. If the fervor of Milton's language or the opaque complexity of Joyce's can be said to mirror the intellectual climate of their times, Franklin's way with words was an almost perfect vehicle for the lucid, reasonable climate of his day.

In pouring over *The Spectator* and in imitating its style, though, Franklin could not have been unmindful of its contents; indeed, its manner was calculated deliberately to complement its substance. In an early paper speaking of his readers, its principal author, Joseph Addison, explained that

> I shall spare no Pains to make their Instruction agreeable, and their Diversion useful. For which Reasons I shall endeavour to enliven Morality with Wit, and to temper Wit with Morality, . . .

and to the End that their Virtue and Discretion may not be short transient intermitting Starts of Thought, I have resolved to refresh their Memories from Day to Day, till I have recovered them out of that desperate State of Vice and Folly into which the Age has fallen. The Mind that lies fallow but a single Day, sprouts up in Follies that are only to be killed by a constant and assiduous Culture. It was said of Socrates, that he brought Philosophy down from Heaven, to inhabit among Men; and I shall be ambitious to have it said of me, that I have brought Philosophy out of Closets and Libraries, Schools and Colleges, to dwell in Clubs and Assemblies, at Tea-Tables and in Coffee-Houses.

Addison's design, then, was to write with enough wit, grace, and liveliness to interest his readers and yet instill in them, without preaching or ranting, the standards of virtue, taste, and morality he thought England needed. The opportunity and need of English letters seemed clear to him. The polemical fanaticism and intolerance characteristic of many Puritan writers had produced the Restoration reactions of reveling in trivia, foppery, and foolishness, of ridiculing morality, decency, and earnestness, and of giving the bawdy, the lewd, and the blasphemous every mark of respect and esteem. Addison meant to be as virtuous as any Puritan without any of their fanaticism and to be as cultured as any courtier of Charles II without any of their decadence, and he succeeded magnificently. He captured his readers, as he captured Franklin, by showing them that their humane and virtuous impulses were wholly compatible with laughter, urbanity, and genial common sense. Imagine the emancipation, the joyous relief, with which a well-disposed youth brought up on stern, scolding sermons would read that "the true

Spirit of Religion cheers as well as composes the Soul; it banishes indeed all Levity of Behaviour; all vicious and dissolute Mirth, but in exchange fills the Mind with a perpetual Serenity, uninterrupted Cheerfulness, and an habitual Inclination to please others, as well as to be pleased in itself."

*The Spectator* taught a moral code strict enough, probably, to suit John Bunyan or Josiah Franklin; it extolled marital fidelity, education, decorum, proper dress, and refined conversation, and abhorred blasphemy, misbehavior in church, dueling, and vulgar superstitions. *The Spectator* castigates playwrights "who want Genius" and are thus reduced to holding their audiences by introducing "a pretty Girl [who] can move lasciviously," and asks instead that authors give delight by appealing to the "good natural Impulses as are in the Audience, but are choaked up by Vice and Luxury." Writers must remember that "a Man that is Temperate, Generous, Valiant, Chaste, Faithful and Honest, may, at the same time, have Wit, Humour, Mirth, Good Breeding, and Gallantry." Thus did *The Spectator* seek to reunite pleasure and virtue. Franklin probably learned from it more than from any other source the urbane attitude which permitted him to benefit from the solid Puritan virtues but without debasing the style of life or ignoring its pleasures as moral zealots are wont to do.

Addison's remarks on public life set an exemplary standard for any youth interested in politics. Speaking of "the Malice of Parties," he deplored the days "when the Feuds ran high between the Round-heads and Cavaliers," and found such disputes "fill a Nation with Spleen and Rancour, and extinguish all the Seeds of Good-Nature, Compassion and Humanity." Instead Addison pleads that we no "longer regard our Fellow-Subjects as Whigs or Tories, but should make the Man of Merit our Friend, and the Villain our Enemy." Though after Franklin entered public life he often engaged in bitter partisan dispute and

was realistic enough to understand that contention
was part of politics, he always viewed such quarrels
as necessary evils and never set out to accomplish
things by creating issues as party leaders often do.
He enjoyed his habitual role as a moderator, a friend
of all parties, in the same mood, though with less
detachment, that *The Spectator* enjoyed his role as
an impartial observer of the passing scene.

Franklin's enthusiasm for *The Spectator* reminds
us of his regret at having spent so much time on the
"Books in polemic Divinity" in his father's library.
In Josiah Franklin's youth, in New England and in
old, the debates over predestination, the authority of
bishops, and the like had a freshness and relevance
in some measure lost fifty years later when his youngest son, Benjamin, read about them. True to the
spirit of *his* age, Benjamin was tired of polemics and
ready for a new approach to the problems of life.
When *The Spectator* showed him that the virtues
he had been taught to cherish could be had without
harangues or fanaticism, his heart leaped and his
mind took a decisive turn. More than any work of
systematic philosophy or any revolutionary world
view, *The Spectator* began Franklin's Enlightenment
and remained throughout his life basic to his mental
outlook. If Franklin's account of his exposure to
books indicates accurately the *order* of his reading
them (and there is every reason to believe this is
so), it is worth noting that his instruction at the
hands of *The Spectator* preceded his conversion to
deism and a utilitarian ethic. Thus his new habit
of mind controlled the nature of his "conversion
experience"; instead of being abrupt and traumatic
and thus conducive to an extreme and fanatic coun-
ter-outlook, it was moderate, easy, and balanced. In
his joy at reading *The Spectator* Franklin shared the
reaction of his contemporaries; its pages display
habits of mind he made his own more abundantly
than the of any other book, and reveal the kind of

Enlightenment he represented so well in word and deed.

Reading *The Spectator* at an impressionable age, Franklin adopted its precepts precisely as Addison would have wished him to do. Thus in a very profound way he took part, perhaps unconsciously, in a "cultural revolution" highly significant for the English-speaking world. He became one of the supreme embodiments of the revival of the classical mood in the British Empire. The new orthodoxy, which Franklin adopted to replace the discarded Puritan one, valued, in F. L. Lucas' words, "light in the brain more than fire in the belly."

After Franklin explained in his autobiography that going on a vegetable diet had made his head clearer and his comprehension quicker, and that he had learned something of mathematics and navigation, he told how he read John Locke's *Essay Concerning Human Understanding* and the Port Royal treatise on logic. Though the *Port Royal Logic or the Art of Thinking* (London, 1687) combined exposure to the traditional syllogisms of Aristotle with instruction in the new inductive procedures of Bacon and Descartes, the usual method of *presenting* or *demonstrating* by the syllogism, proceeding from known propositions to certain conclusions, is often criticized and clearly subordinated to the inductive method, where the main emphasis is on *investigating* and *discovering* truth. The Port Royalists were explicit in saying that understandings verified in experiments had greater weight than logical deductions, however authoritative or profound the latter might seem. Aristotle's deduction that objects fall to the earth with speeds proportional to their weights, then, must give way to the irrefutable observation that swiftness of fall is not related to weight. In short, the Port Royal logic trained Franklin in the crucial new method of inquiry which repudiated all authority not consistent with inductive investigations.* It is significant that Franklin, who habitually confronted his own and other persons' speculations with the dictum "let the experiment be made," had his formal exposure to the art of thinking from a book which extolled *investigation* over *presentation*. His mind was thus turned to the future, not the past.

More significant, and more sophisticated than the schoolbookish text on logic, was Locke's *Essay Concerning Human Understanding* (1690), which revolutionized the prevailing concept of the human mind and how it acquired knowledge. In it Locke rejected the theory, hallowed by Aristotle and the Scholastics, that the mind contained innate ideas, the essence of wisdom and knowledge, which had only to be probed and developed for a man to become learned. Locke held instead that at birth the mind was blank *(tabula rasa)*, and received its furnishings from sense impressions alone. Thus a man in search of knowledge and wisdom must, above all, attend to the impressions made on him by his senses—what he saw, heard, felt, etc. The mind, of course, needed training in order, reasoning, memory, and other skills to best use the data received by the senses, but there was no other beginning except the impressions of the world thus gained. Franklin grew to manhood as Locke's *Essay*, a landmark in the history of thought, was at the peak of its influence. Like most intellectually curious men of his day, Franklin accepted the Lockean understanding of knowledge and its acquisition, and his thought remained within that framework throughout his life.

The implications of Locke's epistemology pervade almost every facet of Franklin's thought. Its fundamental importance to his role as a scientist is ex-

---

* This account of the significance of the Port Royal logic in seventeenth-century English thought is derived from Wilbur S. Howell, *Logic in England, 1500-1700* (Princeton, 1956), pp. 342-63.

plained in Chapter V. Since each mind is pictured as the product of infinitely various sense impressions, infinite points of view must be tolerated, and truth is seen as a changing thing subject to amendment upon discovery of new facts. Applied to public life, Locke's theory of knowledge forbids the divine right of kings, eternal categories setting classes of human beings apart from each other, and obedience to forms and traditions incompatible with changing conditions and aspirations. It abhors superstition in religion and obscurantism in ethics. Locke stated his basic pluralism, which stands behind the demand for human freedom, in a chapter probing the place of power in human affairs:

> . . . the various and contrary choices that men make in the world do not argue that they do not all pursue good: but that the same thing is not good to every man alike. This variety of pursuits shows that everyone does not place his happiness in the same thing, or choose the same way to it. . . .
> Hence it was, I think, that the philosophers of old did in vain inquire, whether *summum bonum* consisted in riches, or bodily delights, or virtue, or contemplation: and they might have as reasonably disputed whether the best relish were to be found in apples, plums, or nuts, and have divided themselves into sects upon it. . . . It is not strange nor unreasonable that men should seek their happiness by avoiding all things that disease them, and by pursuing all that delight them; wherein it will be no wonder to find variety and difference. . . . Though all men's desires tend to happiness, yet they are not moved by the same object. Men may choose different things, and yet all choose right. . . .

Students of American political thought may be surprised to find Franklin remembering Locke's es-

say on the theory of knowledge rather than his
*Second Treatise on Civil Government,* revered in
the United States as the foundation of the Declaration of Independence. Locke wrote the *Second
Treatise* to justify the "Glorious Revolution" of
1688 in England; after that its doctrines were gospel to English Whigs on both sides of the Atlantic.
Since Franklin traveled almost exclusively in Whiggish circles, the key ideas of the *Second Treatise*
—constitutional monarchy, government by consent,
natural rights, and the duty to revolt against tyranny—were axioms to him from his boyhood and did
not need weighty arguments to make them convincing. Though he doubtless knew of the *Second
Treatise,* there is no reason to think he derived
his political principles from it in any direct or
conscious way or even that he ever read it.

It is significant, in fact, that Franklin's earliest
reference to important political writers is to the
famous "Cato's Letters" of Thomas Gordon and
John Trenchard, first printed serially in the *London Journal* beginning in 1720. Franklin quoted from
them in his "Silence Dogood" essays printed in
the *New England Courant* in 1722 and written in
defense of his brother James, then suffering persecution from Massachusetts authorities for alleged
licentious use of his press. "Cato's Letters" trum-
peted the great radical Whig causes—freedom of
speech, the right of government by consent, the
dangers of arbitrary power, the restraints on rulers,
the rights of private property, the threat posed by
a standing army, and all the rest. Like most colonials familiar with the British press and with London pamphlet wars, Franklin learned his political
principles from them rather than from the more re-
mote philosophic treatises upon which they rested.

As a young man, however, Franklin seems to have
been far more interested in what we now call philosophy, religion, and psychology than in government
and social science. The analysis of the human mind

and its liberalizing implications for education and religion concerned him more than politics and economics. After the *Essay Concerning Human Understanding,* he probably read with mounting appreciation Locke's essays on religious toleration, the reasonableness of Christianity, and education. Here were humane comments on many topics under lively discussion in Boston during Franklin's youth: Should those who dissent from an established church be free to worship as they please? Was Christianity as expounded in the Scriptures consistent with reason? Should education of children be rigidly authoritarian or more or less permissive? On these and other topics Locke wrote calmly and convincingly, working out the practical implications of the *Essay Concerning Human Understanding.* In Locke Franklin found a philosopher who wrote about matters of intense personal concern, yet who was at the same time thoroughly conversant with the new scientific view of the world and sympathetic to the Christian and classical traditions.

For Franklin, as for nearly all the men who in America led the movement for independence and who in Europe stood at the front of liberal and reform movements, Locke was the great preceptor, the man who set down views of human nature and society consistent with the winds of change, discovery, and progress which blew so strong in the seventeenth and eighteenth centuries. When Franklin recorded his debt to the English philosopher, he gave himself a place in the mainstream of the intellectual currents of his day and pledged allegiance to the doctrines of toleration and liberty which were its essential characteristics.

Having absorbed so much of the new learning, Franklin turned naturally to the writers who used it to assault orthodox Christianity. He tells us that "from reading [the Earl of] Shaftesbury and [Anthony] Collins, [I became] a real Doubter in

many Points of our Religious Doctrine." Franklin
accepted from the skeptical writers the essential
propositions that there was no necessary connection
between virtue and religion, and that if the two
were found in conflict, reason demanded that virtue
be the more highly honored. As Shaftesbury put it,
the basic inquiry was "what *Honesty* or Virtue is,
consider'd by it-self; and in what manner it is
influenc'd by Religion: How far *Religion* necessarily
implies Virtue; and whether it be a true Saying,
that it is impossible for an Atheist to be Virtuous,
or share any real degree of Honesty, or Merit." To
these questions Shaftesbury answered that virtue
considered by itself was a rational disposition to live
by the natural laws of right and wrong, that religion might help men to so live but that it was not
necessary to such a life, that an atheist could live
virtuously, and that if he did so he was entitled to as
much honor and respect as a man of orthodox
religion who did so.

Shaftesbury and Collins hammered at this theme,
engaged the host of divines who argued for the
*necessary* connection between religion and virtue,
and upheld a natural (we might say humanist)
foundation for the precepts of a good life without
denying that religion was often a useful agency
in helping believers lead a good life. This view, of
course, undercut the orthodox insistence that religion received its sanction from the revelations of
the Scriptures, not from its usefulness in life as
judged by human standards. When Franklin said he
became "a real Doubter," he meant principally that
he accepted the natural ethics of Shaftesbury, Collins, and others. He followed Locke in believing
that

> Nothing that is contrary to, and inconsistent
> with, the clear and self-evident dictates of rea-
> son, has a right to be urged or assented to as a
> matter of faith. . . . Since the precepts of Nat-

ural Religion are plain, and very intelligible to all mankind . . . and . . . revealed Truths . . . are liable to the common and natural obscurities and difficulties incident to words; methinks it would become us to be more careful and diligent in observing the former, and less magisterial, positive, and imperious, in imposing our own sense and interpretations of the latter.

A tract written to refute deism completed Franklin's basic education in religious principles. The treatise, probably Samuel Clarke's *A Discourse Concerning the Being and Attributes of God,* claiming to show rationally "the truth and certainty of the Christian Revelation," had a reverse effect on Franklin: "the Arguments of the Deists which were quoted to be refuted, appeared to me much stronger than the Refutations. In short I soon became a thorough Deist." By this Franklin meant that he rejected the whole structure of miracles, revelations, and literal belief in the Bible which underlay the orthodoxy in which he had been raised, and substituted for it a belief that a deity had indeed made the world in all its marvelous natural harmony and that He did institute laws of order and goodness which a virtuous man was obliged to obey, but beyond that the orthodox creeds and the endless volumes of polemical divinity amounted to very little. They did not, as Franklin said often throughout his life, merit the attention of intelligent men anxious to lead virtuous lives.

For modes of faith let graceless zealots fight;
He can't be wrong whose life is in the right.
POPE, *Essay on Man*

In accepting Locke, Shaftesbury, and the other deists, Franklin's mind took a decisive turn. He abandoned tenets many of his relatives and friends held to be of the utmost importance. In spite of his own unwillingness to let such differences interfere with personal ties, he nevertheless placed himself over a line many people could neither ignore nor forgive. Franklin's respect for his family's religion prevented him from joining the polemicists and iconoclasts and shows how faithful he was to the temper of *The Spectator*. At the same time, however, it is necessary to remember that his own intellectual home was with those his day called the skeptics. In thus blending moderation and tolerance with a belief in new and widely reprobated ideas, Franklin both adopted a characteristic pose and prepared himself to render a valuable service to his country and to mankind: he managed to introduce the new habits of thought, without rancor or convulsion, to many who might otherwise have come by them through the befogging and exacerbating tracts of the controversialists. In his skepticism as in everything else, Franklin insisted upon forbearance, goodwill, and reasonableness.

In adopting deism, Franklin came full circle from the catechisms on which he had been raised and completed his basic education; the habits of mind fundamental to him the rest of his life had been imprinted by the activity and reading thus far described. Since Franklin was not a great innovator in the realm of ideas but rather was notable as one who synthesized and gave effect to the thought of others, it is necessary to see in some detail the sources of his ideas in order then to understand the remarkable uses to which he put them. With a Jonathan Edwards or an Immanuel Kant, who pushes quickly *beyond* what he learns from books to new, seminal thought of his own, it would be proper to devote major attention to the new realms explored. Franklin, though, in fundamentals seldom went beyond the ideas and concepts of his rearing and of his education in the current thought of his day. His mind was eclectic rather than path-breaking. His genius was his ability to apply ideas to the lives of men, his capacity for selecting concepts from his reading and experience to use in particular instances, his judgment of conflicting points of view, and his skill at sensing and pursuing lines of thought relevant to problems at hand. Thus, to understand these fertile *uses* of his mind, we must know first its essential furnishings, the general outlines of which were present in the books and deeds described above.

Over and over again Franklin expressed his admiration and gratitude for the words and examples set before him as a youth. He remembered Cotton Mather in "the vigor of his Preaching and Usefulness," and Mather's *Essays to do Good* gave to his mind "a turn of thinking, as to have an influence on my conduct through life; for I have always set a greater value on the character of a *doer of good,* than on any other kind of reputation; and if I have been . . . a useful citizen, the public owes the advantage of it to that book."

The honor Franklin always showed his father and mother is a clear sign of his debt to traditional Puritan ways. His description of his father in the *Autobiography* is as vivid as it is loving:

I think you may like to know Something of his Person and Character. He had an excellent Constitution of Body, was of middle Stature, but well set and very strong. He was ingenious, could draw prettily, was skill'd a little in Music and had a clear pleasing Voice, so that when he play'd Psalm Tunes on his Violin and sung withal as he sometimes did in an Evening after the Business of the Day was over, it was extreamly agreable to hear. He had a mechanical Genius too, and on occasion was very handy in the Use of other Tradesmen's Tools. But his

great Excellence lay in a sound Understanding,
and solid Judgment in prudential Matters, both
in private and publick Affairs. In the latter indeed he was never employed, the numerous
Family he had to educate and the straitness of
his Circumstances, keeping him close to his
Trade, but I remember well his being frequently
visited by leading People, who consulted him for
his Opinion in Affairs of the Town or of the
Church he belong'd to and show'd a good deal
of Respect for his Judgment and Advice. He
was also much consulted by private Persons
about their Affairs when any Difficulty occurr'd,
and frequently chosen an Arbitrator between
contending Parties. At his Table he lik'd to
have as often as he could, some sensible Friend
or Neighbour, to converse with, and always took
care to start some ingenious or useful Topic
for Discourse, which might tend to improve
the Minds of his Children. By this means he
turn'd our Attention to what was good, just,
and prudent in the Conduct of Life; and little
or no Notice was ever taken of what related
to the Victuals on the Table, whether it was well
or ill drest, in or out of season, of good or bad
flavour, preferable or inferior to this or that
other thing of the kind . . .

On a monument Franklin had erected over his
parents' grave, he wrote that "they lived lovingly
together in Wedlock fifty-five Years; and without
an Estate or any gainful Employment, by *constant
Labour,* and *honest Industry* (with GOD's Blessing)
maintained a large Family comfortably, and brought
up thirteen Children and Seven Grand-children Rep-
utably. From this Instance, Reader, be encouraged
to Diligence in thy Calling, and distrust not PROVI-
DENCE. He was a pious and a prudent Man, she a
discreet and virtuous Woman."

Franklin had a deserved reputation even in his own lifetime as one of the great debunkers of mere preachers and hearers of the Word and as a foe of dogmatism. He was doubtless fortified in these convictions by a remembrance of the cant and hypocrisy he had observed as a boy, and perhaps because he recoiled at his youthful catechizing. His flight from Boston at age seventeen likewise expresses impatience with his family's tutelage. Like many energetic, curious, adventurous men, Franklin would not stay in the small world of his youth. In seeking broader horizons, he was bound to change old ideas as new ones impressed his receptive mind. In moving to the most cosmopolitan city in North America (Philadelphia) and from there to the metropolis of the British Empire, and then to the center of Western culture and civilization (Paris), it is not surprising to find him delighting in new ideas and ways of life.

Yet that he remained essentially a son of New England is apparent in nearly every thought and act of his life. He visited New England frequently and thought occasionally of moving back there, he so much admired the people and their ways. In forming the Junto he used as an example Cotton Mather's neighborhood "improving clubs" in Boston, and the earnest regard Junto members were required to show for each other's well-being and moral growth is reminiscent of Puritan "watch and ward." Franklin's civic enterprises in Philadelphia reflect the Puritan's active concern for social welfare. Poor Richard speaks with an unmistakable Yankee twang. Franklin's political principles, expressed in the mid-1750's in response to Pennsylvania and intercolonial public affairs, have a grassroots character he often ascribed to his familiarity with New England government. In London he enjoyed the company of many Bostonians and very naturally became agent for Massachusetts as her quarrel with the mother country sharpened. His na-

tive sense of Yankee simplicity and directness made
it easy for him to pose in France as a plain Quaker.
When his friends in Boston read his plea for compromise and conciliation at the end of the Constitutional Convention of 1787, they were delighted and
said they saw in it the same man they had known
forty or more years before.

Many critics have argued that at an early age
Franklin purged himself of every trace of Calvinism.
In a theological sense this may be true. The tight
web of doctrine he learned in his catechism and
heard preached over and over again from the pul-
pit of Old South Church he set aside utterly. The
mature Franklin did not believe in original sin, total
depravity, predestination, and other grim, deter-
ministic tenets. The traditional Christian concepts of
sanctification, atonement, and justification by faith,
depending on the miraculous life of Jesus and the
mystical doctrine of the Trinity, did not suit Franklin's habit of mind, though he was no more concerned to dispute the scaffold of doctrine than to
defend it. His mother's fear that he held Arminian
(free will) and deistical views opposed to her Puritan
faith was quite justified, but upon reflection and excepting the moral lapses Franklin himself regretted,
she might have taken a quiet pride in her son's
career. He believed that life was a serious business
to be guided steadfastly toward purposes which
served God and man. He sought constantly to aid
his fellows in the spirit of the Good Samaritan. He
believed that a Providence guided human affairs
and established justice in this life and the next. In
business he aspired to Puritan standards of diligence,
sobriety, and integrity and he regarded his prosperity as a mark of divine favor requiring him to
act as a steward of his wealth for the benefit of
mankind.

It can be argued, of course, that Franklin's moral
views and habits of life are not uniquely Puritan;

that they can be derived from and supported by wholly secular patterns of thought. In fact, the pattern of values often labeled "the Puritan ethic" was not exclusively Puritan even in Franklin's day. Hundreds of conduct and improving books, urging young men to be industrious, thrifty, and prudent to get ahead in the world, had been printed in England during the Tudor and Stuart reigns, many of them written by Anglican or nonsectarian authors. In taking the "simple virtues" to heart, Franklin merely accepted part of the current conventional wisdom. The secular writers he came to admire in his early manhood showed frequently that they, too, valued much of that wisdom. Thus, even though Franklin did adopt new ideas and doubtless would, had he ever taken the trouble, have set down his own systematic philosophy in secular terms, one wonders how much difference the new thought made in the *conduct* of his life. He never rebelled against or repudiated his heritage in the manner of an iconoclast or zealous convert or expatriate. He was always comfortable in his father's house. He showed every mark of respect for his ancestral religion and the men and institutions sustaining it. That he thought and lived as he did, in ways congenial to the habits of his youth, is more reasonably ascribed to those habits than to say that his life rested on ideas he adopted after he had rejected Puritan doctrine. Franklin's earnestness, courage, benevolence, and diligence were the fruits of his father's faith, and those qualities were the wellsprings of his remarkable life, impinging upon his every significant and lasting thought.

Nearly a century after Franklin's death, responding to a claim by Dr. Oliver Wendell Holmes that Franklin's native Boston deserved credit for giving his life its distinctive impetus, Dr. S. Weir Mitchell asserted that Franklin did not begin to live until he breathed the tolerant air of Philadelphia. Nothing

could be farther from the truth. When, in defiance
of his family, he fled to Philadelphia, he knew his
own mind and had acquired the basic principles
which were to guide his life. Moreover, from that
time on, his was primarily a life of action. He was
obliged first to make a living for himself at his
trade and later, having done well at that, his public
duties exacted a heavy toll on his time. Though
Franklin never ceased to search for and welcome
new ideas and more than most men grew mentally
all his life, his attention as a youth to fundamentals
left him with habits of mind he never revised systematically. Rather, he made an amendment here,
an extension there, and continually redefined precepts in the face of altering circumstances. A description of Franklin's mind, then, soon after his
departure from Boston will show us the reservoir
from which he drew the rest of his life.

If, say, during Franklin's first six months in
Philadelphia, he had had long conversations with
some wise and perceptive person who then took time
to set down impressions of the young man, we
might have had drawn the kind of picture we seek.
Most apparent would have been the youth's keenness, alertness, and curiosity. From his jump at age
eight from the middle of his grammar-school class
to its top and from there to the next grade in less
than a year, to his ability when over eighty to
sense ways to accommodate differences at the Constitutional Convention, Franklin was always remarkable for quickness of mind. This showed in the flood
of ingenious proposals he made throughout his life
as well as in the lively conversation which made
him always an engaging companion. Though he was
not a seminal thinker on the order of Descartes or
Newton, Franklin could turn his mind to any subject and see new angles and offer new ideas. As a
young man, this filled him with a self-confidence
often bordering on arrogance. His impulse was to
show his keenness even if this made him ill-man-

nered or offensive or less convincing. At age sixteen and obviously very much a "know-it-all," he wrote biting essays for his brother's paper, the *New England Courant,* satirizing the clergy, magistrates, teachers, and men of wealth in Boston. Some years later in London he wrote a clever, logic-chopping essay to prove that "from the supposed attributes of God . . . *all is right,*" and that therefore there could be neither free will nor blame in men's actions. Franklin soon came to see that such argumentation and self-assertiveness were abrasively self-defeating; learning to outgrow these traits was one of his great triumphs of self-discipline.

Even at the time of our hypothetical conversation, however, Franklin's disciplined and efficient habits would have been apparent. His eagerness to get started in business showed him to be a diligent Puritan lad, not a vagrant, licentious youth. Though his rejection of what he had come to abhor in his training and background was doubtless most vigorous at the time of his flight from home, he never did more than insist upon making his own way in life; he did what he could to maintain honorable ties with his family in Boston. He liked the way things were done in New England, he appreciated the neighborliness of his father's circle of friends, and he respected the earnest purposefulness which pervaded the community. However much he might ridicule the Establishment and satirize its hypocrisy, he generally admired the personal qualities of New Englanders. In a very deep sense he brought to Philadelphia a clear notion of what he admired in human beings; an especially important foundation for one whose life was spent dealing with people, not secluded in a study.

Since Franklin arrived in Philadelphia during a long truce in the Anglo-French warfare, he might not have had occasion to express his conventional patriotism, but the zeal was there, and perhaps like

youths today who devour World War II movies and
tales, his participation in England's past glories was
no less keen for his having come of age after the
fighting was over. His patriotism, though, turned
easily to peaceful, civilizing pursuits. In seizing so
eagerly upon *The Spectator,* he took part in the
movement to "elevate" the cultural life of Britain.
As a colonial, Franklin, like people in Australia or
other far parts of the British Commonwealth or
Empire later on, may have been more zealous in his
"Englishness" even than Addison's circle in London. He had to maintain civilization on the frontier
of the realm where wildness and barbarism would
be quick to take over if not guarded against. As a
boy, after all, Franklin had doubtless heard veterans
of King Philip's War (1675) tell of how narrow
New England's escape from the savages had been,
and when he arrived at Market Street wharf in
Philadelphia, the city was less than fifty years old.
All around him he saw evidence of how close the
English colonies were to a primeval state, and he
responded with a special awareness of the values of
civilization. Thus his patriotism was especially fervent and his enthusiasm for the cultivating mission
of *The Spectator* was especially intense.

Writing to a London printer and bookseller in
1745, Franklin explained in another way the particular regard colonials had for English writers:

> Your authors know but little of the Fame they
> have on this Side the Ocean. We are a kind of
> Posterity in respect to them. We read their
> Works with perfect Impartiality, being at too
> great a Distance to be byassed by the Fashions,
> Parties and Prejudices that prevail among you.
> We know nothing of their personal Failings; the
> Blemishes in their character never reach us,
> and therefore the bright and amiable part strikes
> us with its full Force. They have never offended
> us or any of our Friends, and we have no Com-

petitions with them, and therefore we praise and
admire them without Restraint.

Philadelphia, Franklin was sure, would outdo London and even Edinburgh or Dublin in its zeal for
English culture, and he took a leading part in its
praise and in spreading its leaven throughout the
colonies.

Franklin's practical, enterprising turn of mind,
his ambition to serve himself and his community,
and the free, pluralistic spirit which such enterprise and ambition generate, would have most impressed our hypothetical sage, however. Responding to the unfinished land and beckoning opportunity
all around him, Franklin had a perfect arena in
which to expend his boundless energy. Though the
physical strength, glandular balance, nerve patterns,
and other endowments necessary for this energy
were his by nature's bounty, the *direction* of them
into fields of usefulness and their *organization*
into patterns of accomplishment were from nur-
ture, not nature. Josiah Franklin's son would no
more have wasted talent than he would have wasted
money.

Franklin, an expert swimmer, often urged others
to learn and doubtless taught many to swim. It
would have been criminal, in his view, to withhold
its benefits from mankind. If he could work hard,
apply ideas to practical purposes, and see how to
mold men into institutions, then he was obliged to
act on behalf of himself and his neighbors. More
will be said later about Franklin's political views,
but the fundamentals can be found in this buoyant,
outgoing spirit and the wide scope colonial America offered for its working. When established powers
or entrenched forces of whatever political bias
inhibited enterprise, Franklin opposed them. One
whose mind always moved to the next feasible step,
to a plan for surmounting any particular obstacle,
would be impatient with forms and procedures

which fenced in human ingenuity. Such a person would, in short, be a natural friend of liberty. The life Franklin described in his autobiography comes like dawn before noon in the van of the Declaration of Independence. In a famous epigram acclaiming Franklin, the French philosopher Turgot said "he snatched the lightning from the sky and the sceptre from tyrants." When he arrived in Philadelphia, Franklin's outlook contained the seeds of both deeds.

# Chapter IV

# Business, Personal, and Civic Virtue

FRANKLIN TELLS US that after his first night in Philadelphia, "I made myself as tidy as I could, and went to Andrew Bradford the Printer's." That same day he demonstrated his skill with a printer's composing stick, began to rebuild a press, and undertook to do odd jobs. Since the printers already established in town were "poorly qualified for their Business," Franklin soon convinced leading men in the province that he was a promising young man worthy of support. After his father refused him financial help, Franklin went to London, where for eighteen months he worked hard in the best printing houses and took advantage of the shelves of books available in them. To maintain his strength, he tells us, "I carried up and down Stairs a large Form of Types in each hand, when others carried but one in both Hands." He saved money and kept his head clear by having bread and hot-water gruel instead of beer. He paid for part of his cheap lodgings by helping with the housework. He earned his master's favor by avoiding Monday-morning hangovers and by an "uncommon quickness at composing." He returned to Philadelphia employed by a merchant from whom he learned accounting and soon became "expert at selling." Back at printing,

Franklin instructed the apprentices in the shop, made order out of confusion, invented molds for casting type, and "engrav'd several Things on occasion. I made the Ink, I was Warehouse-man, and every thing, in short quite a Factotum."

On the voyage back to America, Franklin formulated a plan "for regulating my future Conduct in Life. It is the more remarkable," he explained, "as being formed when I was so young, and yet being pretty faithfully adhered to quite through to old age." Though the plan itself has been lost, its principles are doubtless embodied in a memorandum probably drawn during the voyage:

> Those who write of the art of poetry teach us that if we would write what may be worth the reading, we ought always, before we begin, to form a regular plan and design of our piece: otherwise, we shall be in danger of incongruity. I am apt to think it is the same as to life. I have never fixed a regular design in life; by which means it has been a confused variety of different scenes. I am now entering upon a new one: let me, therefore, make some resolutions, and form some scheme of action, that, henceforth, I may live in all respects like a rational creature.
>
> 1. It is necessary for me to be extremely frugal for some time, till I have paid what I owe.
>
> 2. To endeavour to speak truth in every instance; to give nobody expectations that are not likely to be answered, but aim at sincerity in every word and action—the most amiable excellence in a rational being.
>
> 3. To apply myself industriously to whatever business I take in hand, and not divert my mind from my business by any foolish project of growing suddenly rich; for industry and patience are the surest means of plenty.

4. I resolve to speak ill of no man whatever, not even in a matter of truth; but rather by some means excuse the faults I hear charged upon others, and upon proper occasions speak all the good I know of every body.

Though somewhat pompous and smug, these precepts mark out the path to virtue and success, in Franklin's day and in our own, as well perhaps as any statement ever written.

In Philadelphia Franklin soon formed a partnership of his own and began to cultivate goodwill among important men in neighboring provinces. Long nights of work in the print shop and pamphlets printed much more "elegantly and correctly" than those of his competitors convinced officials in Philadelphia that Franklin ought to do their printing. He opened a stationer's shop, and at about the same time he began to issue *Poor Richard's Almanac*, he undertook to emphasize his own devotion to Poor Richard's precepts:

> In order to secure my Credit and Character as a Tradesman, I took care not only to be in *Reality* Industrious and frugal, but to avoid all *Appearances* to the Contrary. I drest plainly; I was seen at no Places of idle Diversion; I never went out a-fishing or shooting; a Book, indeed, sometimes debauch'd me from my Work, but that was seldom, snug, and gave no Scandal; and to show that I was not above my Business, I sometimes brought home the Paper I purchas'd at the Stores thro' the Streets on a Wheelbarrow. Thus being esteem'd an industrious thriving young Man, and paying duly for what I bought . . . I went on swimmingly.

Franklin prospered in his trade and at age forty-two was able to retire under a contract which gave him half the proceeds from his thriving business for twenty more years.

Franklin imbedded the precepts and rules of this "rags to riches" story in *Poor Richard's Almanac,* the source of his first fame and of his greatest reputation around the world. Hence, in his own day and ever since, impressions of Franklin's fabulous career and reactions to the varied output of his pen have been colored by a foreknowledge that all this came from a self-made man who, the more remarkable, had offered thousands, perhaps millions, the keys to his success. He was forever immune from taunts that he did not know anything of the problems of common men or that, as Plato had feared for himself, he would in the end be nothing but a bag of words. He had fought the battles of life faced by the multitudes and he had coined a folklore useful to the fray.

The collection of sayings from *Poor Richard* about thrift, hard work, and prudent management, which first appeared in the *Almanac* for 1758 and which became world famous as "The Way to Wealth," or "La Science du Bonhomme Richard," teaches a very simple lesson: "We are taxed twice as much by our *Idleness,* three times as much by our *Pride,* and four times as much by our *Folly* as by any levy of government." "Sloth maketh all things difficult, but Industry all easy." "What maintains one Vice, would bring up two children." "When you run in Debt, you give to another Power over your Liberty." "Experience keeps a dear School, but Fools will learn in no other, and scarce in that." For a poor boy, ambitious to make his way in the world, they point out what was and still is the clearest, most honorable path. In reducing the lesson to simple homilies, gleaned, as Franklin said, from "the Sense of all Ages and Nations," he made it real to parents and children alike.

The *Autobiography* reinforced the lesson by showing its fulfillment in Franklin's life and by explain-

ing a clever plan for self-improvement. Franklin
tells us that when about twenty, he "conceiv'd the
bold and arduous Project of arriving at moral Perfection. . . . As I knew, or thought I knew, what
was right and wrong, I did not see why I might
not *always* do the one and avoid the other." As always, Franklin's mind moved quickly from the ideal
moral perfection about which philosophers had
long discoursed, to ways and means of achieving it.
He reduced the virtues to thirteen, set them in an
order which permitted those listed first to nourish
the later ones, and then proposed keeping a little
chart on which he marked every departure during
a week from any of the thirteen virtues. Since it
seemed impossible to live up to all of them fully at
the same time, he concentrated on each for a week,
beginning with the first, temperance. Having succeeded at it, he proceeded to the others—silence,
order, resolution, frugality, industry, sincerity, justice, moderation, cleanliness, tranquility, chastity,
and humility. In this way Franklin proposed to complete a "course in virtue" in thirteen weeks and four
in a year. Though he ceased to use the scheme regularly as he advanced in years, he did find that his
faults, more numerous at first than he had supposed,
diminished as he guarded against them. In a moment of honest vanity late in life, Franklin told how
he benefited from the scheme:

> To *Temperance* he [Franklin] ascribes his
> long-continu'd Health . . . to *Industry* and *Fru-*
> *gality,* the early Easiness of his Circumstances
> and Acquisition of his Fortune, with all the
> Knowledge that enabled him to be an useful
> Citizen, and obtain'd for him some Degree of
> Reputation among the Learned. To *Sincerity* and
> *Justice* the Confidence of his Country, and the
> honorable Employs it conferr'd upon him. And
> to the joint Influence of the whole Mass of
> Virtues, even in the imperfect State he was able

to acquire them, all that Evenness of Temper, and that Chearfulness in Conversation which makes his Company still sought for, and agreable even to his younger Acquaintance. I hope therefore that some of my Descendants may follow the Example and reap the Benefit.

Curiously, the adages on frugality and the little scheme for moral perfection have brought upon Franklin a chorus of derision. Nathaniel Hawthorne complained that Poor Richard's proverbs were "all about getting money or saving it," and Herman Melville saw Franklin as full of platitudes, obtrusive advice, and mock friendliness, possessed of a bookkeeper's mind, and altogether of that race of men who were "keen observers of the main chance; prudent courtiers; practical magians in linsey-woolsey." Mark Twain complained of Franklin's "animosity toward boys" in writing about "living wholly on bread and water, and studying astronomy at meal time—a thing which has brought affliction to millions of boys since, whose fathers had read Franklin's pernicious biography." Franklin's most severe critic, D. H. Lawrence, upbraided him contemptuously: "The soul of man is a dark vast forest, with wild life in it. Think of Benjamin fencing it off! . . . He made himself a list of virtues, which he trotted inside like a grey nag in a paddock . . . Middle-sized, sturdy, snuff-coloured Doctor Franklin . . . I do not like him. . . . I can't stand Benjamin [because] he tries to take away my wholeness and my dark forest, my freedom." Brought up on "Poor Richard tags," Lawrence complained that it took him "many years and countless smarts to get out of that barbed wire moral enclosure that Poor Richard had rigged up." Despite Franklin's "good fellowship and occasional good sense," Charles Angoff has charged, he "represented the least praiseworthy qualities of the inhabitants of the New World: miserliness, fanatical practicality, and lack of interest in what are usually known as spiritual things. Babbitry was not a new thing in America, but he made a religion of it."

Some of the charges can be dismissed as absurd. Any man who quits business at forty-two to engage in study and public service, and who makes a career of founding philanthropies, is not a miser. As will be shown later, Franklin did not lack interest in spiritual things, but only in theology and in what he regarded as the stifling of spirituality by moribund or bigoted churches. Though Franklin did keep his own finances in good order, the disgusted remarks of Arthur Lee and John Adams about Franklin's careless bookkeeping while he was minister to France show that he had but a limited inclination to budgets and accounting.

Nevertheless, the charges of the novelists, all in more romantic traditions than Franklin's and all accustomed to deep probing of the human soul, have a certain substance to them. One wonders about a twenty-year-old youth who could write his sister upon her impending marriage, as Franklin did, that he had almost decided to give her "a tea table, but when I considered that the character of a good housewife was far preferable to that of being only a pretty gentlewoman, I concluded to send you a *spinning wheel*." Spinning wheels have their place, especially in the workaday world inhabited by the Franklins of Boston, but a bride deserves more gracious flattery from her brother. At age seventy-six Franklin wrote that "the relish for reading poetry had long since left me," and, though interested in music all his life and the inventor of the harmonica, it is apparent that the mathematical precision of chords, the ingenuity of the instruments, and the classic symmetry of the eighteenth-century masters fascinated him at least as much as aesthetic, intangible qualities. Theodore Parker's observation that "Franklin thinks, investigates, theorizes, invents, but never does he dream" is in some respects a fair assessment.

To do Franklin full justice, though, two further observations are necessary. Just as poets and painters need to eat, poor men enslaved to the drudgery of existence must be taught how in some small way to get ahead of their toil before it makes much sense to speak of their cultural growth, their spiritual grandeur, or their aesthetic tastes. As a tradesman Franklin knew how enervating the daily round of chores could be. As he emerged from it himself, he took the trouble to set down, first in *Poor Richard's Almanac* and later in his autobiography, the precepts which guided him. His own life shows abundantly that he never conceived of the injunctions to industry and thrift as ends in themselves. He knew from experience, though, that they were the simple, obvious habits which could open windows forever shut to men chained, as Thoreau put it, to "lives of quiet desperation." Does a man impoverish life, or enlarge it, by showing men how to open those windows? When millions of men, now as well as in Franklin's day, are caught in the deserts of life without understanding how to get out, is it despicable to show them a way out, however mundane? Franklin is in the first rank of those who have condescended to take men where they are and try to show them the next short step to something better. It is hardly his fault if misguided admirers and myopic critics convert these useful and prudential means into ignoble ends.

Furthermore, a kind of spiritual greatness, a kind of bountiful imagination is required to perform skillfully and harmoniously those responsible functions that make it possible for men to reap the benefits of simple, day-to-day cooperation. Franklin tells us how he took the lead in a London printing shop to achieve better working conditions, and how he tried by example to persuade his co-workers that temperance was to their advantage. His own success in Philadelphia depended heavily on his good relations with leading men in business and politics, and on his initiative in forming the Junto, the library, and other enterprises which showed everyone in town that he could accomplish things working with other people. He formed several successful partnerships with young printers all over British North America, observing that "Partnerships often finish in Quarrels; but I was happy in this, that mine were all carry'd on and ended amicably; owing I think a good deal to the Precaution of having very explicitly settled . . . every thing to be done by or expected from each Partner." Thus, matter-of-factly, Franklin avoided the "little Jealousies and Disgusts [which] arise, with Ideas of Inequality in the Care and Burthen of the Business, etc." Though the stratagem is simple, perhaps even penurious—depending on explicit contracts for business harmony— it is sound advice and it takes a certain amplitude of spirit to see that the harmony thus purchased yields dividends of human felicity those less "lowly" never find.

After long study of the origins of middle-class culture and bourgeois values in Elizabethan England, Louis B. Wright wrote of Franklin as the "supreme expression . . . of American faith in the virtues of industry and thrift." The aphorisms of Poor Richard and the success story of the *Autobiography* are more instructive and more marvelous than the tales of Horatio Alger. Franklin stands with Horace Greeley, Abraham Lincoln, John D. Rockefeller, and Henry Ford as a symbol of what the bourgeois spirit can accomplish, though of course there is little overall resemblance in the careers of these self-made men. Furthermore, Franklin played a crucial role in the development of Western thought when he adapted the earnest piety of his father's home to a secular world and gave his father's habits a utilitarian rather than a theological foundation. He is a prime example of the thesis of Max Weber and others that the Protestant ethic, by insisting on an industrious asceticism, furnishes the cornerstone of commercial civilization. *Poor Richard,* created by one brought up on the *New England Primer,* designed to make youth ambitious for heavenly grace, is a primer for those with worldly ambitions. As we have noticed in speaking of the influence the primers and catechisms and morality stories had on Franklin's lasting habits and values, he transferred from religious to secular objectives readily enough. Franklin's important role in this fateful redirection of human energy is undeniable.

The difficult question, of course, long debated by Franklin's critics, is whether this change has been a "good thing," whether it involves a kind of debasing cynicism which leads straight to the "crass materialism" decried by the prophets of every generation. Those who admire the bourgeois aspect of Franklin's life and thought argue that in turning men's minds from celestial preoccupations, he showed them how to devote their energies to tangible human needs in a world where there was more than enough suffering and deprivation to require all the attention men could give them. They see Franklin, in short, as the practical humanist ever concerned to make the world a better place. One need not boggle if his methods seem devious or impious or neglectful of outmoded moral scruples. On the other hand, Charles Francis Adams, the inheritor of a family grudge against Franklin, wrote that Franklin's ethic "resolves itself into the ancient and specious dogma of *honesty the best policy.* That nice sense which revolts at wrong for its own sake, and that generosity of spirit which shrinks from participating in the advantages of indirection, however naturally obtained, were not his." To those who share this view of Franklin, he seems to show perfectly the fatal consequences of letting religious and moral precepts, valued absolutely as part of a divine law, become mere prudential rules of thumb.

So far as Franklin's own life is concerned, the charges amount to very little. His conduct as a businessman, and later as a politician and diplomat, conformed to the highest standards. He did not, as must happen with those who are honest *only* for utilitarian reasons, become dishonest in his business when it was to his advantage to do so. Franklin did indeed participate in the "advantages of indirection," though a less hostile critic with the same events in mind might have praised him for his tact.

One thinks immediately of the contrasting conduct of Franklin and John Adams in Paris during the American Revolution. Adams, scorning indirection, refused to heed French Foreign Minister Vergennes' advice to conceal his commission to make peace overtures to England until the international situation was more favorable. Franklin thought the advice was sound, or at least, not seeing any particular advantage in immediate disclosure of the commission, he thought it expedient to defer to the French wishes. Adams was indignant and suspicious. He had a commission from his government to deal with the British government; it was demeaning to let Vergennes control that intercourse, especially since he was at that time, in Adams' view, conniving for the benefit of France to keep the United States and Great Britain at odds even after the peace. Adams insisted on being direct, quarreled with Vergennes, and was declared persona non grata. Franklin, on the other hand, remained, behaved deferentially, and kept open the vital flow of French cash and military aid to America. Should Franklin have been more direct? Was he trafficking ignobly in the "advantages of indirection"? In his years in France, as he did constantly through his life, Franklin "stooped" to silence, deference, or flattery when the occasion seemed to demand it, but the record as a whole is one of integrity. As a human being, aside from moral lapses as a youth which he often regretted, Franklin stands as a worthy example in almost every way.

In praising Franklin's life, though, one wonders whether the humanist, utilitarian ethic he espoused in *Poor Richard* and in his autobiography was *really* its basis, and whether, then, his life is proper evidence of the efficacy of such an ethic. As his debt to the childhood training he received in Boston shows, his own habits and character were not formed by the new ethic. It was therefore a kind of rationalization, honest and fitting enough, but it was not the creative force. We may ask legitimately whether the utilitarian ethic would have been as effective in character-building as was Josiah Franklin's faith. Franklin's own children were in some ways worthy human beings, but they had none of their grandfather's zeal nor their father's earnest ambition and steady habits. This fact proves little but it does make one wonder whether there is not some correlation. The habits of everyday life, the worldly qualities which distinguish good men from bad, and the standards of community cooperation are much the same in the Puritan way of Franklin's youth as in the utilitarian system he espoused later. The crux of the matter may be in different degrees of attachment to the principles. The way Franklin learned as a boy had been impressed upon him as a matter of absolutely transcending importance, of life or death everlasting. Thus the habits and values were inscribed deeply.

As a man, on the other hand, he adhered to the new ethical system in a rather abstract, intellectual way, and it is likely he approached his own children with less fervor and insistence than his father had shown toward him. Like many intellectuals of a skeptical frame of mind before and since, Franklin may have been careless in thinking that mankind in general had passions and intentions as well-ordered as his own *had become* under the firm tutelage of Josiah Franklin. In many respects the

point reminds one of the dispute between Shaftesbury and his orthodox opponents over whether virtue
was possible without religion. Shaftesbury's asser-
tion of *possibility,* to which Franklin agreed, seems
sound enough; whether virtue is as *likely* to become
habitual without religion, especially in childhood
training, is another matter. Though Benjamin Franklin's own life demonstrates that the ethic Charles
Francis Adams oversimplified and scorned *could*
be a foundation for greatness and even goodness, a
comparison of his rearing with his own performance
as a parent suggests important differences in the
lasting effects of the two systems.

As a young tradesman in Philadelphia, Franklin
soon extended his concern beyond his own business
affairs and the conduct recommended in the aphorisms he spread abroad so successfully in *Poor Richard's Almanac.* The Junto he formed in 1727 had
as its first purpose the "mutual improvement" of its
members, but they saw their welfare as linked with
that of their community and were soon discussing
questions of civic improvement. They investigated
the causes of success or failure among the business-
men of Philadelphia, bestowed praise on fellow citizens who showed a proper public spirit, encouraged
deserving strangers, proposed beneficial laws, and
sought to guard against "any encroachment on the
just liberties of the people." In short, they strove
"to think of any thing . . . in which the Junto may
be serviceable to *mankind,* to their country, to
their friends, or to themselves." This training in
good citizenship led in Franklin's case to a career
as a civic leader and philanthropist unsurpassed in
the history of Philadelphia and seldom equaled anywhere.

His "first project of a public nature," the library
now known as the Library Company of Philadelphia,
was, Franklin wrote in his autobiography, "the
Mother of all the North American Subscription Li-

braries . . . [which] have improv'd the general Conversation of the Americans, made the common Tradesmen and Farmers as intelligent as most Gentlemen from other Countries, and perhaps have contributed in some degree to the Stand so generally made throughout the Colonies in Defence of their Privileges" during the American Revolution. In appealing for help, the library backers indulged a hope that "Philadelphia [will] be the future Athens of America, [that] plenty of her Sons will arise, qualified with Learning, Virtue, and Politeness for the most important Offices of Life." Franklin's method in founding the library was the same as for all his civic promotions: he saw a need (books were too little available, especially to poor people), consulted with friends, and with them took steps to do something about it. Furthermore, he acted on certain assumptions: that all people could benefit from easier access to books, that an informed public would act for the general welfare, and that knowledge and liberty were inseparable. The rationale for founding the library showed, in short, Franklin's belief in the basic tenets of an open, democratic society.

His other efforts at civic leadership were similarly motivated and similarly successful. He found the city watch conducted irregularly by "ragamuffins" who spent most of the night "tippling," so he undertook a seventeen-year campaign which resulted in a law taxing property to support a punctual watch by responsible officers. To better protect the city against fire, Franklin reminded his fellow citizens that "an Ounce of Prevention is worth a Pound of Cure," observed that "tho' we do not want Hands or Good-will, yet we seem to want Order and Method," and proposed volunteer companies to keep equipment in readiness, practice fire-fighting techniques, and respond immediately to any call of fire in the city. To guard further against the perils of fire, Franklin organized the numerous fire companies into the "Philadelphia Contributorship," the first fire-

insurance company in America. As its first president, he led in formulating policies which set pre-
miums and payments for various losses by fire. The
company suited perfectly Franklin's belief that
"Order and Method" only were necessary to mold
men of goodwill into institutions of common benefit.

To encourage establishment of a college or academy in Philadelphia, Franklin began with a favorite
device: an anonymous pamphlet to set his case before the public and invite others to help and to make
their own suggestions. In *Proposals Relating to the
Education of Youth in Pennsylvania,* Franklin explained why the province needed an academy and
the kind of institution it should be, quoting at length
from Milton, Locke, and other authorities. "The
good Education of Youth," Franklin began, "has
been esteemed by wise Men in all Ages, as the surest
Foundation of the Happiness both of private Families and of Common-wealths." Governments must
assure that "in the succeeding Age . . . Men qualified to serve the Publick with Honour" be properly
trained. In America, where the old leaders educated
in England had died and new ones born and reared
at home would have to take their place, this training
was especially important. He proposed that to keep
the students "in Health, and to strengthen and
render active their Bodies, they be frequently exer-
cis'd in Running, Leaping, Wrestling, and Swim-
ming, etc."

Franklin then began a flank attack on the traditional college curriculum: ". . . it would be well if
[students] could be taught *every Thing* that is useful, and *every Thing* that is ornamental: But Art
is long, and their Time is short. It is therefore pro-
pos'd that they learn those things that are likely
to be *most useful* and *most ornamental,* Regard
being had to the several Professions for which they
are intended." He recommended teaching penman-
ship, drawing, arithmetic, geometry, and astronomy,

but saved his strongest plea for teaching the English
language by studying "our best writers.... Tillotson,
Addison, Pope, Algernon Sidney, Cato's Letters,
etc., should be Classicks: the *Stiles* principally to
be cultivated, being the *clear* and the *concise.*"
Frequent exercise in speaking and in composition
would be the best way to cultivate this skill. Franklin then quoted from Locke and others to show that
exercise in the *mother tongue* was far more efficient in promoting good expression than the hours
spent learning Greek and Latin. He even cited the
ancient authors themselves on their teaching of
their *own* language to develop the style so admired
by the classicists. Franklin's lifelong insistence on
this point has won him a place in educational history,
but it placed him squarely at odds with nearly all
the college leaders of his day.

He urged a full study of history, ancient and
modern, in order, particularly, that the pupils learn
its moral lessons: "... the general natural Tendency
of Reading good History, must be, to fix in the Minds
of Youth deep Impressions of the Beauty and Usefulness of Virtue of all Kinds, Publick Spirit, Fortitude, etc." History would also demonstrate the "wonderful Effects of Oratory, in governing, turning and
leading great Bodies of Mankind, Armies, Cities,
Nations"; and show "the Advantage of a Religious
Character among private Persons; the Mischiefs
of Superstition, etc. and the Excellency of the
CHRISTIAN RELIGION above all others antient or
modern." Historical study would "give Occasion to
expatiate on the Advantage of Civil Orders and
Constitutions, how Men and their Properties are
protected by joining in Societies and establishing
Government. . . . The Advantages of *Liberty,* Mischiefs of *Licentiousness,* Benefits arising from good
Laws and a due Execution of Justice, etc. Thus may
the first Principles of sound *Politicks* be fix'd in the
Minds of Youth." Franklin observed that students
thus acquainted with the past would *want* to learn

Greek and Latin, which should be offered along
with modern foreign languages to those who desired
them or needed them in professional studies.

History did not mean just war and politics to
Franklin, however. He urged the study of customs
and trends in all the lands and societies known to
man, and of natural history, "which would not
only be delightful to Youth . . . but afterwards [be]
of great Use to them, whether they are Merchants,
Handicrafts, or Divines." Natural history would lead
readily to a study of farming. Students might visit
good plantations in the neighborhood: "the Improvement of Agriculture being useful to all, and Skill
in it no Disparagement to any." Commercial history
would also be useful to all students and would produce an interest in mechanics which could then be
taught through demonstration of the wonderful new
machines. Franklin concluded with pleas for "Be-
nignity of Mind" and "Good Breeding," and a hope
that the students would learn what "true Merit"
was: ". . . an *Inclination* join'd with an *Ability* to
serve Mankind, one's Country, Friends and Family;
which *Ability* is (with the Blessing of God) to be
acquir'd or greatly encreas'd by *true Learning*."

The *Proposals Relating to Education* show Franklin at his best, combining traditional practices with
new departures and fusing all together in view of
what was practical under prevailing circumstances.
He was perfectly conventional in placing moral
goals at the apex of his plan, but he proposed to
modernize the subject matter from which students
would learn morality, and he took more direct account than was customary of the various vocations
the students would follow in life. By avoiding any
reference to sectarian religion, he recognized a fact
of life in eighteenth-century Pennsylvania: the di-
versity of religions meant that control by any one
of them would deny the proposed academy the broad
public support it needed to flourish. Though the new
institution was soon dominated by Anglicans, Latin-

ists, and proprietary politicians, and after the first few years Franklin's personal influence in its affairs was almost nil, in the long run it came to serve the purposes he originally intended, and today the University of Pennsylvania rightfully regards him as its founder. It is a monument to Franklin's conviction that benevolence, cooperation, and expanded knowledge are the cornerstones of the good society.

Efforts to found the Pennsylvania Hospital led Franklin to eloquence and to seek again "the advantages of indirection." He first appealed to the public on its behalf:

Among all the innumerable Species of Animals which inhabit the Air, Earth and Water, so exceedingly different in their Production, their Properties, and the Manner of their Existence, and so varied in Form, that even of the same Kind, it can scarce be said there are two Individuals in all Respects alike; it is remarkable, there are none within our Observation, distinguish'd from the rest by this Particular, *that they are by Nature incapable of* DISEASES. The old Poets, how extravagant soever in their Fictions, durst never offend so far against Nature and Probability, as even to feign such a Thing; and therefore, tho' they made their Achilles invulnerable from Head to Foot, and clad him beside in impenetrable Armour, forg'd by the Immortals, they were obliged to leave one soft unguarded Place in his Heel, how small soever, for Destruction to enter at. But tho' every Animal that hath Life is liable to Death, Man, of all other Creatures, has the greatest Number of *Diseases* to his Share; whether they are the Effects of our Intemperance and Vice, or are given us, that we may have a greater Opportunity of exercising towards each other that

Virtue, which most of all recommends us to the
Deity, I mean CHARITY.

Franklin then urged Christians to emulate the
author of their religion and live up to His parable
of the Good Samaritan by binding up the wounds of
the afflicted. Concerned as always to reap the benefits of cooperation, however, Franklin observed that

> ... the Good particular Men may do separately,
> in relieving the Sick, is small, compared with
> what they may do collectively, or by a joint
> Endeavour and Interest. Hence the Erecting of
> Hospitals or Infirmaries by Subscription, for
> the Reception, Entertainment, and Cure of the
> Sick Poor, has been found by Experience ex-
> ceedingly beneficial, as they turn out annually
> great Numbers of Patients perfectly cured, who
> might otherwise have been lost to their Families,
> and to Society.

In the same year (1751) Franklin made this appeal, he became one of the first managers of the
Hospital and acted in the Pennsylvania Assembly to
secure public support. At first economizers and
those who saw no personal benefit from the Hospital
blocked action, but Franklin moved to foil them
by proposing a "matching grant." He offered a bill
pledging £2000 from the Assembly if individuals
subscribed a similar amount.

> This Condition carried the Bill through; for
> the Members who had oppos'd the Grant, and
> now conceiv'd they might have the Credit of
> being charitable without the Expence, agreed to
> its Passage; and then in soliciting Subscrip-
> tions among the People, we urg'd the condi-
> tional Promise of the Law as an additional
> Motive to give, since every Man's Donation
> would be doubled. . . . A convenient and hand-

some Building was soon erected, the Institution has by constant Experience been found useful, and flourishes to this Day. And I do not remember any of my political Manoeuvres, the Success of which gave me at the time more Pleasure. Or that in after-thinking of it, I more easily excus'd myself for having made some Use of Cunning.

Typically, Franklin did not let a delicate sense of propriety balk a stratagem likely to produce results, though in this case his deviousness is hardly an example of the specious doctrine that the end justifies the means. Franklin merely gave his doubting opponents a chance to overcome their own hesitations, and his callous ones a chance to trap themselves in their own wile.

Reviewing two years of operation in a temporary building, Franklin wrote of the feelings of those, doubtless including himself, who had worked on behalf of the Hospital. They knew

> . . . that Satisfaction which naturally arises in humane Minds from a Consciousness of doing Good, and from the frequent pleasing Sight of Misery relieved, Distress removed, grievous Diseases healed, Health restored, and those who were admitted languishing, groaning, and almost despairing of Recovery, discharged sound and hearty, with chearful and thankful Countenances, gratefully acknowledging the Care that has been taken of them, praising GOD, and blessing their Benefactors, who by their bountiful Contributions founded so excellent an Institution.

In Philadelphia Franklin lived on Market Street, where he "saw with Pain the Inhabitants wading in Mud while purchasing their Provisions." Here, and later in London, dirty streets were a persistent challenge to Franklin's civic conscience. "By talking and writing on the Subject," he got a portion of Market Street paved, and some time later persuaded his neighbors to contribute sixpence each month to pay a street sweeper for their part of town. The success of this plan, Franklin thought, "made the People more willing to submit to a Tax for that purpose," and at length Philadelphia had a law (drafted by Franklin) for paving, lighting, and cleaning its streets. He contributed further by designing a ventilated, four-sided street lamp which was less costly to replace and easier to clean than the customary globe. In London, noticing that street dirt flew in shoppers' eyes and covered goods in the stores with dust, to the inconvenience of everyone, Franklin offered a plan for having the streets swept early in the morning, for having the dirt carried away efficiently, and even argued the advantages of single rather than double gutters in narrow streets. He asked those who disdained his concern for such trifles to

. . . consider, that tho' Dust blown into the Eyes of a single Person or into a single Shop on a windy Day, is but of small Importance, yet the great Number of the Instances in a populous City, and its frequent Repetitions give it Weight and Consequence. . . . Human Felicity is produc'd not so much by great Pieces of good Fortune that seldom happen, as by little Advantages that occur every Day. Thus if you teach a poor young Man to shave himself and keep his Razor in order, you may contribute more to the Happiness of his Life than in giving him a thousand Guineas. The Money may soon be spent . . . but in the other Case he escapes the frequent Vexation of waiting for Barbers, and of their some times dirty Fingers, offensive Breaths, and dull Razors. He shaves when most convenient to him, and enjoys daily

the Pleasure of its being done with a good Instrument.

Franklin showed that the earnest goodwill and
zeal to organize and act in the public interest
preached in Defoe's *Essay on Projects* could be
made effective in the life of a great city. No
systematic social theory is apparent, however, in
Franklin's persistent leadership in civic enterprises.
The explanation of his phenomenal success in them,
and his particular genius, lay in his joining of
commonplace precepts with strategies for action.
This outlook and method, quickening our sense of
cooperation and voluntary organization, has become one of the staples mentioned frequently by
analysts of "the American mind." Our Community
Chests, the Red Cross, the associations to alleviate
various diseases, and the countless other undertak-
ings for civic welfare are modern expressions of the
same sense of responsibility that influenced Franklin and his friends in Philadelphia. His accounts of
founding the Library, the Academy, and the Hospital, and of raising funds for them, reflect a timeless humanity and altruism. They show the eclectic
mind of Franklin's day at its best, its energies
channeled by an intense, generous concern for the
general welfare, refusing to bow either to abstrac-
tion or to obstruction.

Though Franklin acted generally as a private
individual in these enterprises, he extended his
activities easily to governing bodies as he entered
politics, and he saw no great theoretical distinction
between private and public action on behalf of human welfare. In fact, Franklin entered public life
largely to enhance his power to act on behalf of
projects he had long supported privately. Thus his
earliest "political theory," his fundamental "public
philosophy," arose from the arena of action marked
out by the Junto objectives set down in 1727. His

first principles were conventional. He accepted, for example, the authority of proprietors and kings in petitioning for their support of the Library or the Hospital or whatever. He worked within the constitutions of Great Britain and of Pennsylvania in his business and community life. At the same time, however, he acquired a firm conviction that the claims of the people's welfare generally had priority over any governing power which sought to thwart them, and he developed great expertise in molding men into institutions, which, when the time came, he would put to use in forming instruments of defiance, rebellion, and nation-building. Philanthropy in Philadelphia, thus, was a superb training for statesmanship.

# Chapter V

# Science

BEFORE DEVOTING HIS energy almost completely to public life, Franklin applied his imagination and his mechanical ingenuity to the thrilling new field of electricity, and thereby gained an international fame which had a great effect on his subsequent career. Amid the excitement over Newton's great synthesis of natural phenomena and the sway of Locke's empiricism, Franklin turned naturally to a fascination with the world of matter and motion around him. While still a teen-ager in London, he met the founder of the British Museum, made friends with Henry Pemberton (Newton's editor and popularizer), and to his lifelong regret barely missed an introduction to Sir Isaac himself. He undoubtedly learned the general principles of the new science in his early devouring of books in Boston, Philadelphia, and London printing shops, and soon applied them in simple ways to everyday problems of his business.

The first notable fruit of his scientific genius, however, was the Pennsylvania fireplace or Franklin stove, invented about 1740 and described in 1744 in a pamphlet typical of Franklin. In thirty-seven pages, Franklin explained the basic principles of heating, showed how the common methods were inefficient because they failed to take advantage of these principles, described the parts and construction of the Pennsylvania fireplace, explained its use, listed fourteen advantages it had, and refuted potential objections to it. The device proved as effective as Franklin's pamphlet was persuasive and soon, first in America and then in Europe, thousands of homes were using it, finding, as Franklin said of his own experience, that "my common room [is] twice as warm as it used to be, with a quarter of the Wood I formerly consum'd there."

The stove and Franklin's pamphlet about it tell us a number of things about his mind. He had read the books of leading scientists on heat theory and understood them thoroughly. His application of their concepts of heat conservation and its transmission by convection as well as by radiation and conduction makes one wonder how such a relatively simple device could have been undiscovered for so long. To "augment the Benefit of Fire," Franklin merely placed the stove farther out in the center of the room and provided two or three more ways for its heat to be used before it went up the chimney. Once again, a strong need (raw Philadelphia winters) combined with a keen understanding resulted in a device enormously helpful to countless numbers of people. Franklin presented the idea unpretentiously, and refused to patent it or profit from it: ". . . as we enjoy great Advantages from the Inventions of others, we should be glad of an Opportunity to serve others by any Invention of ours, and this we should do freely and generously." To him science was like printing and civic organizations, a handmaiden of mankind, good insofar as it enhanced the happiness or well-being of his fellow creatures.

When prosperity permitted Franklin some ease from his business, he turned, as had dozens of curious men all over the Western world, to the new fad of electricity. Some experiments he saw in Boston in 1743 fired his imagination, and soon, with the aid of equipment from England, he began the experiments which made him world famous. Perhaps haphazardly, he read the latest treatises, especially Boerhaave's *Chemistry,* Gravesande's *Natural Philosophy,* and Desagulier's *Experimental Philosophy.* From these books he learned how scientists had pursued the queries Newton had offered in his *Opticks,* and how they had begun to perceive that tiny corpuscles, perhaps like those Newton had postulated to account for light, might be postulated usefully in other areas. At the same time new instruments, especially the Leyden jar, were invented which made many more marvelous and mystifying experiments possible. Thus Franklin and his friends found confusion, flux, and a mood of anticipation as they began their own electrical work. The world awaited reports of new experiments which would fill in gaps of knowledge, but even more it awaited a theory which would explain and systematize all the startling discoveries being made all over Europe. When Franklin offered such a synthesizing idea, explained clearly and logically and supported with ingenious experiments, he won a place beside Newton at a time when men accorded the highest praise to those who unveiled the laws of the physical universe.

A scientific theory, wrote J. J. Thomson, ought "to connect or co-ordinate apparently diverse phenomena, and above all to suggest, stimulate and direct experiment. It ought to furnish a compass which, if followed, will lead the observer further and further into previously unexplained regions." Franklin's work performed this essential function for electricity. When he began his study and experiments, as far as men knew, the static electricity (the only kind known in Franklin's day) produced by rubbing glass with a cloth was nothing more than a weird, insignificant phenomenon unrelated to the great, natural forces of the universe. Though Newton had referred to electricity in passing, he did not include its effects in the physical laws he propounded. When Franklin proved that lightning was a great discharge of static electricity produced by natural movements of air, he placed electricity beside heat, light, and gravity as one of the primordial forces of the universe. Thereafter, "every experimenter rubbing glass tubes in his laboratory knew that he was studying cosmic forces on a small scale."* Lightning's dramatic effects, and the superstitions which had long surrounded it, heightened the awe with which its captor was sure to be held.

Franklin did more than explain a dramatic natural event, however. His theory of electricity, like later theories of Dalton, Max Planck, and Einstein, set forth fundamental postulates about the nature and composition of matter. Franklin's theory in effect proposed for matter a new dimension or quality. He supposed that *all* matter had a certain electrical property and could thus be measured as belonging at some point on an electrical scale going from "positive," or containing an excess of electrical matter, through null, or containing a natural quantity, to a "negative" state containing a deficiency of electrical charge. (The continued use of Franklin's terms "positive" and "negative" to describe charged bodies signifies how important his explanation was.) Thus developed, his theoretical structure had implications for all matter and motion in the universe. The attraction and repulsion of charged bodies was tantalizing evidence that Franklin perhaps had in his hands the keys to the forces which gave cohesion to all substances. In storing greater and greater charges in Leyden jars and in explaining why the charges acted as they did, Franklin seemed to be a kind of master conductor of a physical symphony. Newton had premised a mechanical explanation of

* I. Bernard Cohen, *Franklin and Newton* (Philadelphia, 1956), p. 287. This paragraph, the preceding one, and the following one are derived from Cohen's book, especially pp. 285-94. It is the best book on Franklin as a scientist and should be consulted by students interested in that aspect of his thought.

the universe in terms of attraction and repulsion. Franklin showed how these forces worked in a laboratory just as Newton had explained how they acted in the heavens. Franklin's essential contribution, and the source of the acclaim his work on electricity received in his day, lay in his having enlarged enormously the range of phenomena subject to Sir Isaac's premise, thus confirming the eighteenth-century faith in the harmony of nature.

Franklin's practical imagination moved quickly to probe the worldly uses of his discoveries. He and his friends killed and roasted turkeys with electricity. and tried, with limited success, to cure various forms of paralysis and lameness with electrical shocks. They showed that metals could be fused with static charges and that electricity would pass long distances through water. The most important practical use of the new discoveries, though, was the invention of the lightning rod. Franklin became famous all over the world when the pointed rods soon erected on buildings in Philadelphia, London, and Paris miraculously conducted the powerful discharges safely to the ground. When he harnessed such a previously terrifying and capricious force, his sovereignty seemed to exceed that of the gods and genies of mythology. Franklin put a lightning rod on his own house in 1752, probably saw to their erection on the state house (now Independence Hall) and the Philadelphia Academy building at about the same time, and in *Poor Richard's Almanac* for 1753 described the device for his thousands of readers all over the colonies:

It has pleased God in his Goodness to Mankind, at length to discover to them the Means of securing their Habitations and other Buildings from Mischief by Thunder and Lightning. The Method is this: Provide a small Iron Rod (it may be made of the Rod-iron used by the Nailers) but of such a Length, that one End being three or four Feet in the moist Ground, the other may be six or eight Feet above the highest Part of the Building. To the upper End of the Rod fasten about a Foot of Brass Wire, the Size of a common Knitting-needle, sharpened to a fine Point; the Rod may be secured to the House by a few small Staples. If the House or Barn be long, there may be a Rod and Point at each End, and a middling Wire along the Ridge from one to the other. A House thus furnished will not be damaged by Lightning, it being attracted by the Points, and passing thro' the Metal into the Ground without hurting any Thing. Vessels also, having a sharp pointed Rod fix'd on the Top of their Masts, with a Wire from the Foot of the Rod reaching down, round one of the Shrouds, to the Water, will not be hurt by Lightning.

Though Franklin made significant theoretical contributions in the study of heat, meteorology, and other areas, his energy as a scientist found more characteristic outlet in trying to understand and therefore better cope with troublesome puzzles in the everyday lives of men. By placing pieces of different-colored cloth on snow in the sunshine and then observing how much more rapidly the snow under the darker pieces melted, he furnished a means for measuring what inhabitants of hot climates had long known, that black cloth absorbs heat more readily than white. He devised methods for calming the waves on a pond with oil, but failed when he tried to extend the principle by calming the turbulent waters of the British fleet anchorage at Spithead. By making observations of the times a storm reached different cities along the Atlantic coast of North America, he showed that storms called "northeasters" because of the wind direction in them actually came from the southward. In a series of measurements of water temperature and other phenomena during eight ocean crossings, Franklin furnished the first precise data on the size, direction, and strength of the Gulf Stream. His suggestions for ship design were an early recognition of the advantage fore-and-aft-rigged vessels have over square-rigged ones when sailing to windward. His gadget inventions include bifocal lenses, the armonica, and a device for reaching objects on high shelves, at one time used widely in grocery stores. In every instance Franklin's habit of mind was the same: he noticed a curious phenomenon or a circumstance which bothered somebody, set his mind to understand it, and having done that, exercised his imagination to take advantage of the new knowledge to in some way benefit mankind.

As Franklin's fame spread, curious people sought to learn the secrets of his success as a scientist. In response to one, he wrote:

Your question, how I came first to think of proposing the experiment of drawing down the lightning, in order to ascertain its sameness with the electric fluid, I cannot answer better than by giving you an extract from the minutes I used to keep of the experiments I made, with memorandums of such as I purposed to make, the reasons for making them, and the observations that arose upon them, from which minutes my letters were afterwards drawn. By this extract you will see that the thought was not so much "an out-of-the-way one," but that it might have occurred to any electrician.

Nov. 7, 1749. Electrical fluid agrees with lightning in these particulars: 1. Giving light. 2. Colour of the light. 3. Crooked direction. 4. Swift motion. 5. Being conducted by metals. 6. Crack or noise in exploding. 7. Subsisting in water or ice. 8. Rending bodies it passes through. 9. Destroying animals. 10. Melting metals. 11. Firing inflammable substances. 12. Sulphureous smell. The electric fluid is attracted by points. We do not know whether this property is in lightning. But since they agree in all the particulars wherein we can already compare them, is it not probable they agree likewise in this? Let the experiment be made.

Careful observation and shrewd suggestion of hypothesis were important, but the final five words were the real foundation of Franklin's discoveries. He followed no line of reasoning further than the experiments in his laboratory would permit. When he came upon difficulties he could not resolve, he urged a candid acknowledgment. To a request for an explanation of a curious phenomenon Franklin had described, he replied:

... You require the reason; I do not know it. Perhaps you may discover it, and then you will be so good as to communicate it to me. I find a frank acknowledgment of one's ignorance is not only the easiest way to get rid of a difficulty, but the likeliest way to obtain information, and therefore I practice it: I think it an honest policy. Those who affect to be thought to know every thing, and so undertake to explain every thing, often remain long ignorant of many things that others could and would instruct them in, if they appeared less conceited.

Early in his work Franklin set down the contribution electrical study made to his mental outlook: "In going on with these Experiments, how many pretty Systems do we build, which we soon find ourselves oblig'd to destroy! If there is no other Use discover'd of Electricity, this, however, is something considerable, that it may *help to make a vain Man humble.*"

Franklin's care about not making unwarranted projections from his experiments and his willingness to discard unsound hypotheses did not prevent his sharing the eighteenth-century confidence that man would someday unlock all the mysteries of the universe. He wrote Joseph Priestley in 1780 that:

> ... the rapid Progress *true* Science now makes, occasions my regretting sometimes that I was born so soon. It is impossible to imagine the Height to which may be carried, in a thousand years, the Power of Man over Matter. We may perhaps learn to deprive large Masses of their Gravity, and give them absolute Levity, for the sake of easy Transport. Agriculture may diminish its Labour and double its Produce; all Diseases may by some means be prevented or cured, not excepting even that of Old Age, and our lives lengthened at pleasure even beyond the antediluvian Standard.

Though these miracles and many more have come to pass since Franklin's day, we do not share his easy optimism about their benign meaning. Nuclear holocaust, fallout, germ warfare, concepts of a darkening solar system, and the monstrosities which sometimes trail behind life-saving chemicals and drugs leave us skeptical of nature's benevolence. As some of Franklin's scientific work has been proved too simple, so his understanding of the forces at work in the world strikes us as naïve. As an eighteenth-century philosopher, he dwelled in some measure in "the heavenly city," where, following Newton's lead, he expected to see all mysteries revealed as parts of a harmonious universe. More will be said later about Franklin's place in the eighteenth-century climate of opinion. We need observe now only that his accomplishments as a scientist gave him a much sounder understanding of the physical foundations of that climate than was true of many of his illustrious contemporaries, and that his fame as an electrician gave to his personality and way of life a universal appeal which was an essential part of his thought and mind during the last forty years of his life.

Sir Humphry Davy summarized Franklin's outlook and contribution as a scientist:

A singular felicity of induction guided all his researches, and by very small means he established very grand truths. The style and manner of his publication are almost as worthy of admiration as the doctrine it contains. He has endeavoured to remove all mystery and obscurity from the subject; he has written equally for the uninitiated and for the philosopher; and he has rendered his details amusing as well as perspicuous, elegant as well as simple. Science appears in his language in a dress wonderfully decorous, the best adapted to display her native loveliness. He has in no case exhibited that false dignity, by which philosophy is kept aloof from common applications, and he has sought rather to make her a useful inmate and servant in the common habitations of man, than to preserve her merely as an object of admiration in temples and palaces.

# Chapter VI

# Politics

IN COLONIAL AMERICA printing was very much a public business. Nearly all those who succeeded at it were printers for some agency of government and many held a variety of public offices. Shortly after Franklin entered his first partnership, he printed without charge or commission an address of the Pennsylvania Assembly which had been done carelessly by William Bradford, the official printer. The members, Franklin tells us, "were sensible of the difference: it strengthened the Hands of our Friends in the House, and they voted us their Printers for the year ensuing [1730]." From then on Franklin printed the statutes and minutes of the Assembly. He became so intimately acquainted with its business and many of its members that in 1736 he was chosen its clerk and thereafter, of course, attended its meetings.

During the same years he began his career as a propagandist on public affairs. He wrote a treatise favoring paper currency at a time when trade in the province flourished but was threatened by a lack of a circulating medium. Franklin showed that an expansion of credit could provide an important stimulus to the economy, and that the real wealth of a country depended on the value of the improvements produced on its land and in its shops rather than on the amount of specie accumulated. He had in mind the general well-being of the colony, not the special class interest of debtors and workers, as some have supposed. Although some creditors, especially those interested in debts owed in England, opposed the currency expansion, Governor Patrick Gordon and apparently most of the merchants large and small supported it. The Assembly soon passed a currency measure and as a reward later employed Franklin to print its money: "... a very profitable Jobb and a great help to me. This was another Advantage gain'd by my being able to write."

Franklin also sought to enlighten the public through his newspaper, *The Pennsylvania Gazette:*

> I considered [it] ... as another Means of Com-
> municating Instruction, and in that View fre-
> quently printed in it Extracts from the Specta-
> tor and other moral Writers. ... I carefully
> excluded all Libelling and Personal Abuse. ...
> Whenever I was solicited to insert any thing of
> that kind, and the Writers pleaded as they gen-
> erally did, the Liberty of the Press ... my
> Answer was, that I would print the Piece sep-
> arately if desired ... but that I would not
> take upon me to spread his Detraction, and that
> having contracted with my Subscribers to fur-
> nish them with what might be either useful or
> entertaining, I could not fill their Papers with
> private Altercation in which they had no
> Concern without doing them manifest Injustice.

Such prudence, not always adhered to strictly though the *Gazette* was far more decorous than many colonial newspapers, increased Franklin's standing with the leading men of the province. Furthermore, the important place carrying news-papers had in the mail service helped him become postmaster in Philadelphia in 1737, and in 1753, by dint of several strategic applications, he received ap-pointment from the crown, with William Hunter, as deputy postmaster general for North America.

Thus Franklin's trade, by affording natural and
profitable entries to public affairs, opened a wider
arena in which he might exercise his community
spirit. He did not enter public office until 1748, the
year of his retirement from business, and he was not
elected to the Pennsylvania Assembly, the real sign
of his political maturity, until 1751. By then his
newspaper, almanac, and philanthropy had made
him one of the best-known men in the province, his
post-office work and business had acquainted him
with important people all over the colonies, and his
scientific papers had introduced him to influential
men abroad. Franklin did not enter politics as a
crusader or instigator of "bloodless revolution" in the
affairs of the province. He took his seat with the help
of established Quaker leaders and in order to sponsor
further community projects he had supported earlier
as a businessman and citizen.

Before he entered the Assembly, Franklin played
a key role in a fascinating political dilemma. Through
prudence, humanity, and good luck, Quaker politicians in Pennsylvania had managed to maintain an
official policy of pacifism for over fifty years. The
province had no army, no militia, no forts, and no
wars with the Indians. In 1747, however, war between France and Great Britain brought French
privateers into Delaware Bay, but pacifism para-
lyzed the Assembly even in the face of attacks by
armed vessels within thirty miles of Philadelphia.
When many citizens (the Quakers were no longer
a majority in Pennsylvania) demanded action, the
province faced an ugly situation: civil violence
might ensue if French attacks grew more bold and
the government still refused to build forts or form
a militia. In a pamphlet, *Plain Truth*, Franklin
urged a face-saving solution. Let the Quaker government, on the whole a good one, preserve its pacifist
principle by passing no law, but let the people who
wanted to take up arms form a voluntary militia
(with officers elected by the ranks as was done in

New England) and raise money to build a fort.
The proposal was an instant success. For the first
time armed men marched in the streets of Philadelphia. Though no attack occurred before hostilities
ceased the following summer, the fact of military
preparation was an event of major importance.

When the crisis ended, Franklin was a hero to all
but the strictest pacifists and the most bellicose
patriots. He had enabled the province to defend
itself without asking the Quakers to do what they
could not: use the force of law to compel their conscientious brethren to pay war taxes or serve in the
militia. In pointing out the compromise course,
Franklin displayed anew to Philadelphians the habit
of mind they had come to expect from him. He
might have joined with the zealous patriots, among
whom were many of his Junto friends, to use the
fear of French guns to undermine Quaker power
in the province. Instead he sought the low road of
accommodation, assured himself of support by mod-
erates on all sides, and earned the enmity of every
variety of extremist.

Strict Quakers condemned him for seducing their
brethren from the pacifist principle, while the Proprietor of Pennsylvania, Thomas Penn, saw in
Franklin's activity another kind of danger: "This
[militia] Association is founded on a Contempt
to Government, and cannot end in anything but
Anarchy and Confusion . . . [Franklin] is a dangerous Man and I should be very Glad he inhabited
another Country, as I believe him of a very uneasy
Spirit. However as he is a Sort of Tribune of the
People, he must be treated with regard." Though
Franklin had undertaken the defense activity as
innocently as he had many other civic enterprises,
at its conclusion he was just what the canny, ap-
prehensive Thomas Penn feared: a popular leader
inclined to place the claims of public welfare above
those of any hereditary power or even of the edicts
of government itself if necessary. In 1748, though,

he did not doubt that the British and Pennsylvania
constitutions provided the best and freest government in the world, and that good men had but
to act together under them to achieve whatever the
community required.

Franklin took his seat in the Pennsylvania Assembly in 1751 in full sympathy with the oligarchy
of Quaker merchants and farmers that had been
dominant for over fifty years. As in any free
society, there had been bitter political disputes
throughout Pennsylvania history, but until the
1750's, Quaker power had proved unassailable.
Franklin thought them not nearly as stubborn on
the subject of defense as their opponents alleged,
and in providing honest government, sound financing,
good Indian relations, and support for worthy projects, he found them among the ablest rulers anywhere; "good and useful Members" who ought not
to be ostracized because some of them (a minority,
Franklin thought) were pacifists.

Long before 1751, trouble had been in the wind
over the role the proprietors should play in the
province's affairs. Originally William Penn had acted
like the benevolent manager of a large estate, col-
lecting revenues (quitrents) but also contributing
in many ways to the support of the colony. Since
in this special role he often returned more to the
province than he took from it, his lands and enterprises were exempt from ordinary taxation. His
sons, though, principally Thomas, had little interest
in the Quaker experiment, were absentee landlords,
and came more and more to think solely in terms of
the profit they could derive from the province. As
Thomas Penn set his affairs in order, and began to
make money from his vast lands in Pennsylvania, the
Assembly thought it only fair that he help support
the government, ultimately by paying taxes on his
lands. Franklin accepted the Assembly argument

and first stated his own political principles in its
behalf. When Thomas Penn and his allies in Pennsylvania stubbornly and resourcefully defended every
proprietary prerogative, the conditions were set
for the contest in fundamentals of government which
reached a climax in 1776, though of course Franklin
had no thought of independence when in 1755 he
pondered the iniquity of the proprietary tax exemp-
tion.

Before the contest with the proprietors reached its
height, Franklin again displayed his zeal for defense
of the British realm (and incidentally emphasized
his standing as Pennsylvania's most resourceful citizen) by finding wagons, when no one else could,
for Braddock's ill-fated expedition against Fort
Duquesne in 1755. He used his well-known name and
good credit to recruit 200 or more wagons from
farmers, mostly Pennsylvania Germans, who responded to his shrewd combination of offering a
chance to make extra cash and of veiled threats of
impressment and punishment if Braddock did not get
the wagons he needed. After Braddock's defeat,
Franklin took the lead in Pennsylvania in seeking
money for defense and in organizing to oppose attacks by French and Indians all along the frontier.
In persuading the Quaker leaders in the Assembly
to support large defense expenditures, he declared
his wholehearted support for their campaign to tax
the proprietary estate, all the more just and necessary, he thought, since the money would be used to
defend their lands as well as everyone else's.

Meanwhile, for the only time in his life, Franklin
accepted military commissions; he built forts on the
exposed frontier and commanded the Philadelphia
militia, organized under a law he had drafted and
guided through the Assembly. By the spring of
1756 he was at the peak of his personal power, ac-
cused by his foes of being a dictator and demagogue,
but heralded by a friendly poet:

Who bid Yon Academick structure rise?
"Behold the man!" each lisping babe replies.
Who schemed Yon Hospital for the helpless poor?
And op'd to charitable use each folding door.
Our Countrys cause, what senator defends?
Void of all partial, or all private ends.

In a moment of vanity Franklin wrote simply of his
acclaim: "The People happen to love me."

As penman for the Assembly, though, Franklin
engaged in a long and increasingly bitter war of
words with the governors of Pennsylvania, especially Robert Hunter Morris, whose tenure of less than
two years (1754-56) was one of the most tumultu-
ous in the history of the province. He was a re-
doubtable and unflinching opponent, highly skilled
in invective as well as in dialectic, and engaged
Franklin and the Assembly with enthusiasm. In
months of angry exchanges, Morris goaded Franklin
to a rancor he seldom displayed in public or private.
After recounting the rights and privileges which he
held the Assembly enjoyed because of its British
heritage and which Morris had denied could be so
derived, Franklin turned on the governor:

In one Thing, indeed, it is our Misfortune,
that our Constitution differs from that of England. The King has a natural Connection with
His Subjects. The Crown descends to his Posterity; and the more his People prosper and
flourish, the greater is the Power, Wealth,
Strength and Security of his Family and Descendants. But Plantation Governors are frequently transient Persons, of broken Fortunes,
greedy of Money, without any Regard to the
People, or natural Concern for their Interests,
often their Enemies, and endeavouring not only
to oppress but to defame them, and render them
obnoxious to their Sovereign, and odious to their
Fellow Subjects. Our present Governor not

only denies us the Privileges of an English Constitution, but would, as far as in his Power, introduce a French one, by reducing our Assemblies to the Insignificance of their Parliaments, incapable of making Laws, but by Direction, or of qualifying their own Gifts and Grants, and only allowed to register his Edicts. He would even introduce a worse; he requires us to defend our Country, but will not permit us to raise the Means, unless we will give up some of those Liberties that make the Country worth defending; this is demanding *Brick without Straw,* and is so far *similar* to the Egyptian Constitution. He has got us indeed into *similar* Circumstances with the poor Egyptians, and takes the same Advantage of our Distress; for as they were to perish by Famine, so he tells us we must by the Sword, unless we will become Servants to our Pharaoh, and make him an *absolute Lord,* as he is pleased to stile himself *absolute Proprietary.*

Could Pennsylvania change its governor as easily as it could its Assembly (elected annually), Franklin wrote at another time, it would "deserve much less the character which he gives it, of an unfortunate Country." The personal bitterness of these exchanges belies Franklin's bland account in the *Autobiography* of his political career in Pennsylvania and shows that he responded, as men who take public life seriously often do, with heat and passion when the occasion required.

In the midst of these angry charges, a piece appeared in the *Pennsylvania Journal* which, if not written by Franklin, had his approval and summarized his reasons for opposing the proprietors:

The people of this Province are generally of the middling sort . . . chiefly industrious Farm-

ers, artificers, or Men in Trade; they enjoy and
are fond of Freedom, *and the meanest among
them* thinks he has a Right to Civility from the
greatest . . . the Representatives of the People
having the Right of disposing of the People's
Money, granting Salaries, and paying Accounts
. . . are of Course a respectable Part of the Government. And as they are to be chosen annually,
the common People whose Votes are so frequently necessary in Elections, are generally better
treated by their Superiors on that Account. . . .
Hence the People are commonly attach'd to
the Assembly, and jealous of its Privileges and
Independency, as knowing that their own Freedom and Happiness, and the Publick Wellfare,
depend on the Support of those Privileges, and
that Independency. . . . [We believe] that all
the Powers in Possession of the Assembly
are necessary to the Publick Wellfare . . . that
Assemblies more rarely misuse their Power than
Governors, their Interest and that of the
Publick being one and the same . . . that an
Increase of Offices and of Fees to be paid by
the People, is an Increase of Burthen. to no
Purpose; an Impoverishment of the Inhabitants,
and weakening of the State. . . . That if the
Proprietor's Influence over the Assembly is so
increas'd, as that they are render'd dependent
and subservient to his Pleasure, it may as well
be left to him to make the Laws, Assemblies
thenceforth will be Cyphers; they will be worse
than Cyphers, they will become the Instruments
of Oppression. . . . That Elections by private
ballot, are fairest, and best show the free Inclination and Judgment of the People; and
that if Persons in Power, and those who are
called *Gentlemen*, will take care to increase in
Virtue as they do in Wealth, they can never fail
of sufficient Respect from the People.

Franklin's prescription that the ills of proprietary rule be cured by seeking a royal government for Pennsylvania shows that he had no elaborate, systematic natural-rights theory in mind in opposing the proprietors. He began with a practical judgment, based on twenty-five years of deep involvement in the affairs of the province, that an increase in proprietary power would inhibit the power of Pennsylvanians to deal with their problems in ways best suited to them. Thus he exalted the authority of an assembly which had long discharged faithfully its public trust, ridiculed proprietary privilege, and defended honest elections. These were but the simple precepts of Poor Richard, of common sense, fair play, and concern for the commonweal, applied to government. Franklin doubtless knew the precepts agreed with the doctrines of Locke and other natural-rights theorists, just as he knew his readers were well versed in those theories. But nothing is plainer, in Franklin's ever-growing commitment to public life, than the inductive approach his experience made possible: he sought laws which would account for and deal with the circumstances and conditions he knew existed among his friends and neighbors.

At the time Franklin entered politics, he revealed, in his soon-to-be-famous hoax "The Speech of Miss Polly Baker," the reasonableness of his view of public affairs. He satirized the severe laws of New England for punishing women who had illegitimate children by composing a plea he alleged a woman who had broken one of those laws had addressed to the court convicting her:

This is the Fifth Time, Gentlemen, that I have been dragg'd before your Court on the same Account; twice I have paid heavy Fines, and twice have been brought to Publick Punishment, for want of Money to pay those Fines. This may have been agreeable to the Laws, and I don't dispute it; but since Laws are sometimes

unreasonable in themselves, and therefore repealed, and others bear too hard on the Subject in particular Circumstances; and therefore there is left a Power somewhat to dispense
with the Execution of them; I take the Liberty
to say, That I think this Law, by which I am
punished, is both unreasonable in itself, and
particularly severe with regard to me, who have
always lived an inoffensive Life in the Neighbourhood where I was born, and defy my Enemies (if I have any) to say I ever wrong'd
Man, Woman, or Child. Abstracted from the
Law, I cannot conceive (may it please your
Honours) what the Nature of my Offence
is. I have brought Five fine Children into the
World, at the Risque of my Life; I have maintain'd them well by my own Industry, without
burthening the Township, and would have done
it better, if it had not been for the heavy
Charges and Fines I have paid. Can it be a
Crime (in the Nature of Things I mean) to
add to the Number of the King's Subjects, in a
new Country that really wants People? I own
it, I should think it a Praise-worthy, rather
than a punishable Action. . . . But, how can
it be believed, that Heaven is angry at my
having Children, when to the little done by me
towards it, God has been pleased to add his
Divine Skill and admirable Workmanship in the
Formation of their Bodies, and crown'd it, by
furnishing them with rational and immortal
Souls. Forgive me, Gentlemen, if I talk a little
extravagantly on these Matters; I am no Divine, but if you, Gentlemen, must be making
Laws, do not turn natural and useful Actions
into Crimes by your Prohibitions. . . .

Though Franklin doubtless had humor more in
mind than moralizing or social criticism in this
hoax, its spirit, condemning any law which af-

fronted common sense and which led to pernicious
or ridiculous results, is wholly consistent with his
utterly serious public philosophy.

In fact, we may view Franklin's appearance on
the public stage as the culmination of a nearly
perfect education in citizenship. As a boy he had
been trained to be a good person, to honor what
was right and just, and to concern himself with
the welfare of others. As a businessman and civic
leader in Philadelphia he learned lesson after lesson in human relations. Every undertaking from
the Junto to the Pennsylvania Hospital gave him additional experience in transforming goodwill and
zeal into effective institutions. His work as a
scientist dramatized the principles common to scientific investigation and to human affairs in an open
society. When he entered politics, he simply undertook to extend his activities to the area where at
age fifty he might best exert his energies. The oath of
the Athenian citizen, doubtless known to Franklin,
states precisely the obligation this background led
him to assume unhesitatingly: "We will ever strive
for the ideals and sacred things of the city, both
alone and with many; we will increasingly seek to
quicken the sense of public duty; we will revere
and obey all the city's laws; we will transmit this
city, not less but greater, better and more beautiful
than it was transmitted to us."

Unlike most colonial politicians, Franklin from
his first year in the Assembly took a leading part in
intercolonial affairs. As a businessman with connections from Halifax and Boston to Charleston and
Antigua, as a printer with a newspaper and almanac
which circulated throughout the colonies, as postmaster general, as a member of the universal brotherhood of science, and as a patriot with a grand
concept of the British Empire, Franklin turned
readily to the common interests and problems of all

the English plantations in the New World. As if to lay a firm foundation for nearly twenty-five years of devotion to the expansion of the British Empire, in 1751 he wrote *Observations Concerning the Increase of Mankind, Peopling of Countries, etc.* Starting from the proposition that there is "no Bound to the prolific Nature of Plants or Animals, but what is made by their Crowding and interfering with each others Means of Subsistence," Franklin asserted that the natural increase in population in the colonies, if not hampered by restrictive laws, was sure to exceed that common in Europe and would greatly enhance British power. In another century, the doubling of population in every generation which happened in the colonies would leave "the greatest Number of Englishmen . . . on this Side of the Water. What an Accession of Power to the British Empire by Sea as well as Land! What Increase of Trade and Navigation! What Numbers of Ships and Seamen!" He found the economic prospects just as alluring: ". . . in proportion to the Increase of the Colonies, a vast Demand is growing for British Manufactures, a glorious Market . . . which will increase in a short Time even beyond [Britain's] Power of supplying, tho' her whole Trade should be to her Colonies: Therefore Britain should not too much restrain Manufactures in her Colonies. A wise and good Mother will not do it. To distress, is to weaken, and weakening the Children, weakens the whole Family."

Franklin explained further that the increase of population in the colonies would be rapid because early marriages, encouraged by easy expectations of raising children, would produce families two or three times as large as those common in Europe. The vast expanses of land would encourage thrift and industry, which in turn would encourage large families, just as in Europe cities spawned luxury and idleness, which made large families expensive. Luxury, said Franklin, "tends to diminish the

Families that indulge in it, who are few. The greater
the common fashionable expence of any Rank of
People, the more cautious they are of Marriage.
Therefore Luxury should never be suffer'd to become common." He thought the effects of slavery
wholly pernicious; its introduction "greatly diminish'd the Whites . . . the Poor are by this Means
depriv'd of Employment, while a few Families
acquire vast Estates. . . . The Whites, who have
Slaves, not labouring, are enfeebled, and therefore
not so generally prolific; the Slaves being work'd too
hard, and ill fed, their Constitutions are broken, and
the Deaths among them are more than the
Births. . . . Slaves also pejorate the Families that use
them; the white Children become proud, disgusted
with Labour, and being educated in Idleness, are
rendered unfit to get a Living by Industry." Franklin concluded his analysis by extolling the superiority
of the Anglo-Saxon race. When the British stock
had such a high rate of natural increase, "why
should the Palatine Boors [German peasants] be
suffered to swarm into our Settlements? . . . Why
should Pennsylvania, founded by the English, become a colony of *Aliens?*" Franklin then appealed
to Englishmen to keep the complexion of America
fair: the rest of the world was sufficiently "black
and tawney"; let the British colonies be a place
of Anglo-Saxon genius flourishing in all its glory.*

This perceptive essay, quoted approvingly by
Thomas Malthus and admired by demographers ever
since, had a wide geopolitical influence in its own

---

* Though Franklin's ethnocentrism seems bigoted today,
for his time it was exceedingly mild. In fact he was far
ahead of most Britons in recognizing the virtues of other
races and nationalities. He praised the humane habits of
American Indians, scorned the theory that Negroes were incapable of education, and later urged that immigrants be
welcomed in America solely with regard to their merit and
enterprise.

day. First printed in Boston in 1755, it was reprinted immediately in London, and within a year
appeared in *Gentleman's Magazine* and other British
periodicals. In the debates over the nature of the
British Empire which preceded the American Revolution, it received repeated attention. It urged, in
persuasively simple terms, that the Empire be
dynamic, deriving its strength from growth, trade,
and enterprise, rather than from restrictive regula-
tion or inhibiting alliances. Franklin was sure that
given the opportunity to expand and develop, the
energy of Englishmen on both sides of the Atlantic
would soon extend British influence to the four
corners of the earth. The Empire thus flourishing,
quarrels within it would be submerged, and united,
it would easily overmatch any combination of enemies. Like ancient Athens, Franklin saw Britain as
the "school for all the world," her benign power and
influence spreading because of the clear proof she
gave in her deeds and ways that she had something
useful to give to other people. Though he clothed his
analysis in the conventional garb of British patriotism and national superiority, his fundamental devotion was to the progress of mankind.

The moral content of Franklin's expansionism is
abundantly clear in his dream of establishing English colonies in the Ohio Valley. From its natural
advantages, he argued, the region "must undoubtedly
. . . become a populous and powerful dominion; and
a great accession of power, either to England or
France." But beyond the geopolitical considerations,
Franklin wrote exuberantly to his esteemed friend
the evangelist George Whitefield, proposing that by
combining their talents they could render a great
service to mankind: "What a glorious thing it
would be, to settle in that fine Country a large
Strong Body of Religious and Industrious People!
What a Security to the other Colonies; and Advantage to Britain, by Increasing her People, Territory,
Strength and Commerce. Might it not greatly fa-

cilitate the Introduction of pure Religion among the
Heathen, if we could, by such a Colony, show them
a better Sample of Christians than they commonly
see in our Indian Traders, the most vicious and
abandoned Wretches of our Nation?"

Whitefield's preaching and his own exposition of
Poor Richard's sturdy qualities, Franklin thought,
would put the essential stamp of virtue on an expansionism otherwise demanded by British power
politics. Franklin accepted joyously what another
age would call "the white man's burden." He believed that his mother country (England) did indeed
lead the forces of progress and goodness in the
world, and that an expansion of her domain would
result in more plantations of freedom and prosperity
such as those already flourishing along the Atlantic
coast. Since at this time he sensed no tyranny as a
British subject, albeit a colonial one, he did not
conceive that an enlarged empire would be oppressive to any part of the realm.

The dark shadow of France in the Ohio Valley,
falling across the paths of Pennsylvania and Virginia traders there by 1750, threatened to upset
Franklin's vision of empire, and precipitated his
first acts as an intercolonial statesman. At the
Albany Congress of 1754, under the motto "Join or
die," he urged a colonial union in order better to
face the French threat, deal with the Indians, and
protect trade. He proposed a loose federation com-
prised of a "Grand Council" to be chosen by the
assemblies of the various colonies and a "President
General" to be appointed and supported by the King
and empowered to veto acts of the Council, or if he
approved, to execute them. Franklin propounded no
great theory of union nor did he say anything about
colonial rights of self-government. He simply proposed what to him were the obvious steps Great
Britain and the colonies had to take together if they
were jointly to survive and flourish. In defending

the plan, he pointed out the difficulties of voluntary cooperation among the colonies: "some assemblies [are] at variance with their governors or councils . . . others [take] the opportunity, when their concurrence is wanted, to push favourite laws, powers, or points that they think could not at other times be obtained, and so [create] disputes and quarrels," and so forth. Furthermore, "one principal encouragement to the French, in invading and insulting the British American dominions, was their knowledge of our disunited state, and of our weakness arising from such want of union." Therefore, to the practical Franklin, a union was necessary.

The plan foundered on colonial bickering and British unwillingness to encourage any measures increasing the power of colonial legislatures, but in the year before his death, after the federal constitution of 1787 had been adopted, Franklin commented on the failure of the Albany Plan: if it, "or something like it, had been adopted and carried into Execution, the subsequent Separation of the Colonies from the Mother Country might not so soon have happened. . . . The Fate of this Plan was singular. . . . The Crown disapproved it, as having plac'd too much Weight in the democratic Part of the Constitution; and every Assembly as having allow'd too much to Prerogative. So it was totally rejected."

When a royal governor proposed that the colonial assemblies be excluded from any power in the Union, Franklin outlined for him the objections that would be made to the exclusion and at the same time set down, in December, 1754, attitudes pregnant with meaning for the future:

. . . That the People in the Colonies, who are to feel the immediate Mischiefs of Invasion and Conquest by an Enemy, in the Loss of their Estates, Lives and Liberties, are likely to be better Judges of the Quantity of Forces necessary to be raised and maintain'd, Forts to be

built and supported, and of their own Abilities
to bear the Expence, than the Parliament of
England at so great a Distance. . . .

That it is suppos'd an undoubted Right of
Englishmen not to be taxed but by their own
Consent given thro' their Representatives. That
the Colonies have no Representatives in Parliament. That to propose taxing them by Parliament, and refusing them the Liberty of
chusing a Representative Council, to meet in
the Colonies, and consider and judge of the
Necessity of any General Tax and the Quantum,
shews a Suspicion of their Loyalty to the Crown,
or Regard for their Country, or of their Common Sense and Understanding, which they
have not deserv'd. That compelling the Colonies
to pay Money without their Consent would be
rather like raising Contributions in an Enemy's
Country, than taxing of Englishmen for their
own publick Benefit. That it would be treating
them as a conquer'd People, and not as true
British Subjects. . . .

As we are not suffer'd to regulate our Trade,
and restrain the Importation and Consumption
of British Superfluities, (as Britain can the
Consumption of Foreign Superfluities) our whole
Wealth centers finally among the Merchants
and Inhabitants of Britain, and if we make them
richer, and enable them better to pay their
Taxes, it is nearly the same as being taxed
ourselves, and equally beneficial to the Crown.
These Kind of Secondary Taxes, however, we
do not complain of, tho' we have no Share in
the Laying or Disposing of them; but to pay
immediate heavy Taxes, in the Laying Appro-
priation or Disposition of which, we have no
Part, and which perhaps we may know to be
as unnecessary as grievous, must seem hard
Measure to Englishmen, who cannot conceive,
that by hazarding their Lives and Fortunes in

subduing and settling new Countries, extending
the Dominion and encreasing the Commerce of
their Mother Nation, they have forfeited the
native Rights of Britons, which they think
ought rather to have been given them, as due
to such Merit, if they had been before in a
State of Slavery.

This mixture of patriotism, economics, and common sense served as the basis for Franklin's view
of the British Empire as long as he retained his
allegiance to the King of England.

Permitted to fulfill their bright destiny, the
American colonies could become a source of strength
which would make the empire invincible. Not worried
by the increased independence which would come
with greater strength, Franklin could look with
excitement at the prospect of the colonies out-
growing the mother country. Ministers in London,
except the elder William Pitt and a few others who
shared Franklin's vision, could see only that as the
colonies grew, the need to control them became at
once more pressing and more difficult. As a resident
of the new world, impressed every day with its
boundless growth, Franklin was utterly convinced
that his homeland had a splendid destiny, bountiful,
free, and progressive. Heir to the tradition of Cabot,
Raleigh, Drake, John Smith, the Pilgrims, William
Penn, and a host of others, he did not conceive at
first that this destiny might come to being under
any but the English flag. He expected Britain to be
"a wise and good Mother," attentive to the needs
of the whole family. But just as the seeds of independence are visible in his opposition to the proprietors as a member of the Pennsylvania Assembly,
his belief in the irresistible expansive power of the
American colonies was sure to overcome allegiance
to British rule if he were ever convinced that that
rule was unchangeably hostile and oppressive to
what Jefferson called "the Empire of Liberty."

It is significant, though perhaps accidental, that
the part of Franklin's growth of mind thus far
described, down to his period of nearly thirty years'
residence in England and France, is the part he
recounted in his famous autobiography. With engaging clarity and freshness, this book shows how
Franklin came to be the man he was, prosperous,
famous, and at the peak of his powers, upon his
departure for England in 1757. In an obvious way,
the book is incomplete; Franklin's long service as
agent in England, minister to France, and revolutionary sage is not described. In another way,
though, the book is complete in that it has reached
the climactic point in Franklin's life. In it we are
told how the poor Boston boy, brought up by pious
Puritan parents, learned a trade, ran away from
home, adopted some unorthodox beliefs, succeeded
in business, wrote folklore for a generation in *Poor
Richard's Almanac*, rose to be Philadelphia's first
citizen, acquired world fame as a scientist, became
a popular political leader, and developed a grand,
expansive vision of Britain's imperial destiny. Viewed
beside the memoirs of soldiers and noblemen which
filled English bookshops in his day, recounting deeds
of valor on the battlefield and finesse in the boudoir,
Franklin's autobiography is a most extraordinary
document indeed. So, too, the habits of mind outlined
above, remarkable enough in any day, in Franklin's
were downright revolutionary.

Franklin's experience and inventive mind had
defined a whole outlook which in a twinkling seemed
to outmode apparently timeless and eternal patterns
of life. Though one may argue justly that Franklin
rode rather than generated the expansive forces of
his day, still his life was the beacon which showed
what the forces could mean to men everywhere. His
was not the first poor-boy-makes-good success story,
but he was the first to make the odyssey seem
credible and to set down the precepts which had

made it possible—and which presumably could make
it possible for other diligent youths.

Equally significant, Franklin had rendered his
energy and his passion for accomplishment effective
in his community. A mere printer, a runaway of
whose family nothing was known in Philadelphia,
he found resources enough within himself and a
sufficiently open society to make a decisive impact
on the life of the city. The confidence this experience
generated, and the conviction thus acquired that the
earth belonged to *all* the living for the general benefit
of *all* mankind, were the primeval revolutionary
forces which found dramatic expression in 1776.
After one reads Franklin's autobiography and real-
izes that its author had lived in Boston and Philadelphia between 1706 and 1757, the events of 1763-89
in America seem much less startling. Franklin *was*
the new man of the new world, in flesh and blood
telling his own story in words clear to all, over whom
philosophers in the old had merely speculated and
marveled.

When Franklin went to England in 1757, his
political foes were frightened. "Considering the
popularity of [Franklin's] character and the reputation gained by his Electrical Discoveries . . .
he may prove a Dangerous Enemy," wrote Richard
Peters, Thomas Penn's agent in Pennsylvania. His
skill and craft as a politician, gained in his innumerable "intrigues" in Philadelphia, might even
"effect a change of Government." Penn, used to the
traditional ways of English rule, responded con-
fidently: "Mr. Franklin's popularity is nothing here
. . . he will be looked very coldly upon by great
People . . . who are to determine the Dispute between us." Aided by ministers whose ways he had
judged very well, Thomas Penn for nearly twenty
years thwarted Franklin's mission to pull down proprietary government in Pennsylvania, but in the
long run Peters' fears were proved well founded.

Franklin's character and philosophy of life, attuned to the ways of his country, showed a resilience which led in time to independence, and the courtly, privileged system of Proprietor Thomas Penn fell into such utter oblivion that today few remember that he held almost feudal power in Pennsylvania for over thirty years.

Thus, in assessing Franklin's thought, one may fairly say that as its outlines were visible in the education he received in Boston, its mature quality was apparent after thirty years of vigorous activity in Philadelphia. The great achievements and writings of his later life but fulfill the commitment and promise of his first half century. His later scientific work was what one would have expected from the author of *Observations and Experiments in Electricity*, published in 1751. His calm, confident, well-informed appearance before the House of Commons in 1766 would not have surprised his neighbors in Philadelphia, however dumfounded English gentlemen were at the smooth performance of the colonial tradesman. His indignation at Lord North's repressive, bribing insolence just before the American Revolution would not have startled his fellow apprentices in Boston, who had seen him bridle under the petty tyranny of his brother James. Those who had seen his tactical skill in a dozen civic enterprises in Philadelphia would have expected him to be the equal of Louis XVI's wily foreign minister during years of negotiations in Paris. The author of a dozen successful propaganda campaigns in the *Pennsylvania Gazette* was well trained to write such barbed masterpieces as *An Edict by the King of Prussia* or *Rules by Which a Great Empire May Be Reduced to a Small One*. The bagatelles Franklin wrote to amuse his friends in Paris were but the wit of Poor Richard clothed in elegance and given feminine airs. Whatever Franklin did or wherever he went after leaving Philadelphia in 1757, he re-

mained the new man of the new world. That he did
so is the secret of his remarkable success.

As an old man, hobbled with gout and bladder
stone but full of wisdom, he had frequent occasion to
review the deeds and doctrines of his middle years
as Philadelphia's first citizen. In nearly every instance he confirmed earlier judgments and positions.
In 1789, against the renewed attacks of the classicists, he continued to favor the practical plan of
education emphasizing studies in English he had
offered in 1749. His faith in scientific progress never
wavered. When confronted with skepticism about
the value of the lighter-than-air balloon flown in
Paris in 1783, he replied, "Of what use is a new-born
babe?" At the Constitutional Convention of 1787
he espoused, not always successfully, precepts of
government he had found worked well during the
1750's: a unicameral legislature, frequent and secret
elections, and limited offices of profit under government. His old-age opinion of the wisdom of the
Albany Plan has already been noted. Franklin was
not unusual in having reached settled habits of
thought by his fiftieth birthday. He was unusual,
however, in his opportunity to act effectively on behalf of those convictions in his old age and in seeing
so many of them gain wide sway in many parts of
the world. The opportunity was his in large measure
because the habits of mind visible in his autobiography were the habits of freedom and enterprise which
were the wave of the future.

# Chapter VII

# Vision of Empire: From
# Loyalty to Revolution

WHEN FRANKLIN REACHED England in the summer
of 1757, seeking relief from what he regarded as
the tyranny of proprietary government, leading
Quakers took him to see Lord Granville, president
of the Privy Council and a power in English politics
since the days of Robert Walpole. Though cordial,
the meeting between the haughty lord and the
tradesman-agent must have been a strange one.
During the conversation they probed the basic issues
which more and more were to divide mother country
and colonies during the next twenty years. Granville asserted that "you Americans have the wrong
Ideas of the Nature of your Constitution; you
contend that the King's Instructions to his Governors
are not Laws, and think yourselves at Liberty to
regard or disregard them at your own Discretion.
But those Instructions . . . are first drawn up by
Judges learned in the Laws; they are then considered, debated and perhaps amended in the Council, after which they are signed by the King. They
are then, so far as relates to you, the *Law of the
Land*, for THE KING IS THE LEGISLATOR OF THE COLO-
NIES." Franklin replied that "this was new Doctrine
to me. I had always understood from our Charters,
that our Laws were to be made by our Assemblies,

111

to be presented indeed to the King for his Royal
Assent, but that being once given the King could
not repeal or alter them. And as the Assemblies
could not make permanent Laws without his Assent, so neither could he make a Law for them without theirs. He assur'd me I was totally mistaken. I
did not think so however. . . . His Lordship's Conversation a little alarm'd me."

During the French and Indian War, the quarrel
between royal ministers and colonial agent lay dor-
mant, but Franklin's letters to his friends in Pennsylvania leave little doubt that he soon learned of the
hazards American interests faced amid the devious
ways of British politics. Lord Hardwicke, next to
Granville in power on the Privy Council, was for
carrying the royal "Prerogative higher in all Respects even on this side of the Water." Since they
governed the Council, Franklin reported, "one may
easily conjecture what Reception a Petition concerning Privileges from the Colonies may meet with"
there. The Board of Trade, the body which exercised
what direct administration the colonies received
from London, offered no more hope. At Franklin's
first appearance before the Board, its president, Lord
Halifax, denounced Franklin's fellow agent, Robert
Charles, for "improper, indecent . . . arrogant,
insolent behaviour." Charles's offense had been to
ask, as a matter of *right,* for full access to papers on
a case before the Board relating to Pennsylvania.
Only William Pitt, the speaker of the House of
Commons, and Attorney General Charles Pratt were
"staunch Friends to Liberty." Under the circumstances, Franklin thought an appeal to the House
of Commons more propitious; many members were
"Friends of Liberty and noble Spirits, yet a good
deal of Prejudice still prevails against the Colonies.
The Courtiers think us not sufficiently obedient."

At the same time Franklin had the utmost respect
for Pitt as a war leader and as a virtuous politician.
His "steady and disinterested conduct" had rescued

Britain from the ministry of corruption presided over
by the Duke of Newcastle and was the "principal
Foundation of Hope" for success in the war with
France.

His universal Character of Integrity is what
gave him his present Power, rather than the
Favour of the King which he had not, or Party
Interest which was little more than popular
Esteem and Opinion. Men of abilities were in
the Ministry before, but one of that kind
seem'd to be wanting for a Center of Union,
who was, or at least was generally believ'd to
be, an HONEST MAN. Measures proposed by a
Man of abilities without Honesty, are always
suspected, and he becomes weak thro' the Diffidence of those that should concur with and
help him; but the Man of moderate Talents
who is believ'd to mean well, and to act up-
rightly for the common Good, has everyone's
ready Assistance, and thereby is able to do
more than the other of superior Parts: But
when Ability and Integrity meet in the same
Person, his Power of doing Good must be
greater, as he can himself plan right Measures,
will receive all necessary Advice, can distinguish
what is good, and can have all the necessary
Assistance in the Execution.

In "going home," as Franklin and other colonials
called a journey to England, he had not the slightest
doubt that the government there would deal with
him justly and compassionately. He believed the
Whig propaganda of seventy years' duration: the
British Constitution of King, Lords, and Commons
was the best and freest in the world. As his attitude
toward Pitt showed, Franklin thought it needed
only to be in the hands of virtuous men to deserve
the most complete loyalty. But his "alarm" at
Granville's theory of colonial rule and his strictures

on other lords who held high notions of the royal
prerogative demonstrate that he also saw the partisan nature of British politics. His role, then, and
the key to success, he thought, would be to work
with the Whiggish, liberal group, to nourish their
power if he could, and to use their influence in
promoting the objectives of his agency. Thus admiring the Constitution and accepting the ministerial
system which operated under it, Franklin needed
finesse and tactical skill, not thunderbolts of protest
and theories of dissent, to succeed in his mission.
For nearly all his eighteen years as a colonial agent
in England, he acted as a loyal subject, encouraging
what he thought best in her intentions and system
of government.

First frustrated and then moderately successful
in his effort to get the proprietors to pay taxes and
otherwise relinquish some of their privileged position in Pennsylvania, Franklin also devoted much
of his energy and imagination to the affairs of the
empire at large. He exulted in the triumphs of
Amherst and Wolfe and saw clearly that their conquest of Canada meant his dream of a great Anglo-
Saxon dominion in North America might be fulfilled.
When politicians, thinking of affairs in Europe and
heedless or fearful of the expanding empire in
America, proposed returning Canada to France in
exchange for Guadaloupe in the West Indies, Franklin responded with his most ambitious inquiry into
British imperial destiny.

Amid an analysis of the economic value of Canada
as compared with that of Guadaloupe and assessments
of the military advantages of possessing each, Franklin hammered home his manifest destiny theme.
Guadaloupe, a valuable sugar-producing island already populated with Frenchmen and their slaves,
was worse than useless in the grand scheme of expanding English peoples and influence: "A country
*fully inhabited* by any nation is no proper possession

for another of different language, manners and religion. It is hardly ever tenable at less expense than it is worth." Canada in French possession, on the other hand, inhibited the existing English colonies, and prevented English enterprise from opening vast tracts of fertile wilderness to cultivation and civilization, thus restricting the opportunity of English manufacturers as well as of American pioneers. "A people spread through the whole tract of country, on this side the Mississippi, and secured by Canada in our hands, would probably for some centuries find employment in agriculture, and thereby free us at home [in England] effectually from our fears of American manufactures."

Franklin wrote to the Scottish philosopher Lord Kames of the boundless prospects:

No one can more sincerely rejoice than I do, on the reduction of Canada; and this is not merely as I am a colonist, but as I am a Briton. I have long been of opinion, that the *foundations of the future grandeur and stability of the British empire lie in America;* and though, like other foundations, they are low and little seen, they are, nevertheless, broad and strong enough to support the greatest political structure human wisdom ever yet erected. I am therefore by no means for restoring Canada. If we keep it, all the country from the St. Lawrence to the Mississippi will in another century be filled with British people. Britain itself will become vastly more populous, by the immense increase of its commerce; the Atlantic sea will be covered with your trading ships; and your naval power, thence continually increasing, will extend your influence round the whole globe, and awe the world! If the French remain in Canada, they will continually harass our colonies by the Indians, and impede if not prevent their growth; your progress to greatness will at best be slow, and give room for many accidents that may forever prevent it.

At the same time Franklin sought to reassure those who feared that American growth might lead to separation or might threaten the mother country. Would the colonies, unable to unite in the face of the dire threat from France, unite against "their own nation, which protects and encourages them, with which they have so many connexions and ties of blood, interest, and affection? . . . when I say such an union is impossible, I mean without the most grievous tyranny and oppression. People who have property in a country which they may lose, and privileges which they may endanger, are generally dispos'd to be quiet, and even to bear much rather than hazard all. While the government is mild and just, while important civil and religious rights are secure, such subjects will be dutiful and obedient. The waves do not rise but when the winds blow." No more suspecting Lord North's measures of 1774 than did his readers, Franklin did not intend a threat but rather sought to make rebellion seem absurd by arguing that only impossible measures could produce it.

During the Great War for Empire which ended in such dramatic English victory, no Briton except William Pitt himself exceeded Franklin in his vision of expansive empire. When he found brilliant leadership of the war in London and also managed to attract very influential support to his campaign against the proprietors, it is not hard to see why his fervor as an Englishman and his attachment to the mother country increased during the early years of his residence in England. When he returned to Philadelphia for eighteen months in 1762-64, he continued to urge rescue from proprietary tyranny by seeking what he believed would be the easy yoke of royal rule. He had full confidence in the power and inclination of the House of Commons to protect English liberties on both sides of the Atlantic.

Perhaps even more important, Franklin had come to love his English friends: "Of all the enviable things England has, I envy it most its People. Why should that petty Island, which compar'd to America, is but like a stepping-stone in a Brook, scarce enough of it above Water to keep one's Shoes dry; why, I say, should that little Island enjoy in almost every Neighbourhood, more sensible, virtuous, and elegant Minds, than we can collect in ranging 100 Leagues of our vast Forests? But 'tis said the Arts delight to travel Westward. You have effectually defended us in this glorious War, and in time you will improve us. After the cares for the Necessaries of Life are over, we shall come to think of the Embellishments." Five years in London drawing rooms and in country houses all over the British Isles had demonstrated that there were personal and cultural bonds between the colonies and mother country, as well as economic and political ones. Thus, though Franklin had sensed a danger in Lord Granville's conversation and had unintentionally warned of the course which would drive the colonies to rebellion, he began his long residence "at home" in a burst of British patriotism, full of pride in her standing as a world power, and devoted to her people and culture.

In the ten years between Franklin's second journey to England as provincial agent in the winter before the Stamp Act was passed (1765), and his return to Pennsylvania in the same month as the battles of Lexington and Concord (April, 1775), he played a leading role in the long, pulsating debates over the government of the empire. He knew more about America than any Englishman and more about England than any American. As the gulf between mother country and colonies widened, he became agent for one colony after another, and was looked to as their common spokesman. One can view the ten years of intense concern and incessant writing on Franklin's part in many ways. In the first place, he helped formulate the successive American responses to objectionable British measures. Before the House of Commons he expounded the distinction between external taxes such as duties on trade, which he said Parliament could lay, and internal taxes such as the stamp levy, which he alleged abridged the right of no taxation without representation. Though the distinction quickly proved specious, it helped for a time to define a basis for agreement. He also debated the respective powers of Parliament and the Crown in governing the colonies, and he wrote at length on whether the colonies were or should be content with "virtual representation" in Parliament. On these constitutional questions Franklin fought effectively for American rights, but he did not have a legalistic mind and did not think attention to nice points of law was as important as preserving the essential right of self-determination he had believed in ever since he could remember.

Franklin sought also to gain specific points in disputes between particular colonies and the mother country. He presented petitions, delivered remonstrances, interviewed ministers, advised colonial legislatures, whispered to members of Parliament, and wrote anonymous articles in the press. He thus knew intimately the merits of dozens of quarrels and had abundant opportunity to see, in the clear light of particular examples, which side most often had right or honor or fair play on its side. In this task he stoutly defended American rights, but often counseled his countrymen to be patient, and in instances such as the Boston Tea Party, where he thought they had acted too rashly, he advised them to make retribution. Applying the moderate, practical habits of mind which were second nature to him, Franklin worked diligently for conciliation throughout the trying ten years. The best evidence that

he sought accommodation and even compromise are
the charges brought against him by extremists on
both sides: intemperate Americans thought him "soft
on England" while British ministers abused him for
being too outspokenly American.

The real struggle in Franklin's mind, however,
was not over constitutional principles or the merits
of particular disputes. He would have accepted almost any legal formula or modus vivendi that would
have preserved American self-determination within
the empire. He wanted good government that would
permit widest scope for the human fulfillment he had
experienced in America. Franklin's great mental
trauma was to come to believe, slowly but surely,
that this fulfillment could not take place as long as
he and his countrymen were subjects of George III.
An account of this realization records a crucial
change in Franklin's political convictions and at
the same time shows how Americans came to justify
their rebellion against the mother country.

Though Franklin very nearly forfeited his political
career by assuming the Stamp Act would be obeyed
in America and by having a political ally appointed
stamp agent in Pennsylvania, he nevertheless worked
for its repeal, which he hoped would strengthen the
bonds of empire. "Our Friends here," he wrote
from London, "are in Pain, lest the Condescension of
Parliament, in repealing the Stamp-Act, will encourage the Americans to farther Excesses; and
our Enemies, who have predicted it, hope to see their
Prophecies fulfilled, that they may disgrace the
present Ministry; but I hope we shall behave prudently, and disappoint them, which will establish
the Ministry, and *thereby effectually secure* the
American Interest in Parliament. Indeed I wish this
Ministry well, for their own Sakes, as well as ours,
as they appear to me to be really very honest worthy
Men, with the best Intentions. . . ."

In the next year (1767), following the fall of the

friendly ministry and as passage of the Townshend Acts seemed imminent, Franklin wrote Lord Kames of his forebodings:

I have lived so great a part of my life in Britain, and have formed so many friendships in it, that I love it, and sincerely wish it prosperity; and therefore wish to see that Union, on which alone I think it can be secured and established. As to America, the advantages of such a union to her are not so apparent. She may suffer at present under the arbitrary power of this country; she may suffer for a while in a separation from it; but these are temporary evils that she will outgrow . . . America, an immense territory, favoured by Nature with all advantages of climate, soil, great navigable rivers, and lakes, etc., must become a great country, populous and mighty; and will, in a less time than is generally conceived, be able to shake off any shackles that may be imposed on her, and perhaps place them on the imposers. In the mean time, every act of oppression will sour their tempers, lessen greatly, if not annihilate the profits of your commerce with them, and hasten their final revolt; for the seeds of liberty are universally found there, and nothing can eradicate them. And yet, there remains among that people, so much respect, veneration and affection for Britain, that, if cultivated prudently, with kind usage, and tenderness for their privileges, they might be easily governed still for ages, without force, or any considerable expence. But I do not see here a sufficient quantity of the wisdom, that is necessary to produce such a conduct, and I lament the want of it.

After Parliament had passed the Townshend Acts and American nonimportation agreements in protest

were known in England, Franklin explained the
causes of American discontent in an English newspaper: "It has been thought wisdom in a Government exercising sovereignty over different kinds of
people, to have some regard to prevailing and established opinions among the people to be governed.... This had been the wisdom of our Government with respect to raising money in the Colonies. It
was well known, that the Colonists universally were
of opinion, that no money could be levied from
English subjects, but by their own consent given
by themselves or their chosen Representatives. . . ."
In the face of this opinion, if not to say right,
Parliament nevertheless imposed taxes on the colonies
and they resisted, peacefully but firmly. For so
doing, Franklin observed, Americans "have been
reviled [in Parliament] as *Rebels* and *Traitors* . . .
we [are] separated too far from Britain by the
Ocean, but we are united to it by respect and love,
so that we could at any time freely have spent our
lives and little fortunes in its cause: But this unhappy new system of politics tends to dissolve those
bands of union, and to sever us for ever."

A few months later, in May, 1768, during riots
over the imprisonment of the radical leader John
Wilkes, Franklin grew alarmed that conditions might
make a connection with England a liability: " . . . all
respect to law and government seems to be lost
among the common people, who are moreover continually inflamed by seditious scribblers, to trample
on authority and every thing that used to keep them
in order. . . . [They exhibit] a universal sullenness,
that looks like a great black cloud coming on, ready
to burst in a general tempest. . . . The ministry,
divided in their counsels . . . have for some years
past had little time or inclination to attend to our
small affairs." Between 1765 and 1775, Franklin's
hope for union depended more on his judgment of
conditions in *England* than on news from America;
Westminster, not Boston or Williamsburg, was for

him the scene of critical and ominous events. Though he still abhorred the thought of disunion, he had, eight years before the Declaration of Independence, affirmed his faith in American capacity to thrive should that unwelcome event take place, and pointed to the acts and attitudes in London which would lead to it.

After repeal, in April, 1770, of all the Townshend duties except that on tea, Franklin hoped anew that the colonies might remain within the empire, but at the same time he expressed a disillusionment with the virtue and goodwill of Parliament which was as crucial to his changing attitude as it was to that of Jefferson and John Adams: "Let us . . . hold fast our Loyalty to our King, who has the best Disposition towards us, and has a Family Interest in our Prosperity; as that steady Loyalty is the most probable means of securing us from the arbitrary Power of a corrupt Parliament, that does not like us, and conceives itself to have an Interest in keeping us down and fleecing us. . . . I think, that, except among those with whom the spirit of Toryism prevails, the popular Inclination here is, to wish us well, and that we may preserve our Liberties." A year later, however, as agent for Massachusetts, Franklin saw "the seeds of a total disunion" in new measures against that colony. Petty tyrannies by greedy officeholders would lead to bursts of outrage and violence by the people, which would in turn cause "severe punishments . . . inflicted to terrify. . . . Thence the British nation and government will become odious, the subjection to it will be deemed no longer tolerable; war ensues, and the bloody struggle will end in absolute slavery to America, or ruin to Britain by the loss of her colonies; the latter most probable, from America's growing strength and magnitude."

In 1772 Franklin returned from a trip to Ireland

and Scotland with a fresh impression of American
virtue:

> I thought often of the Happiness of New
> England, where every Man is a Freeholder, has
> a Vote in publick Affairs, lives in a tidy, warm
> House, has plenty of good Food and Fewel,
> with whole cloaths from Head to Foot, the
> Manufacture perhaps of his own Family. . . .
> If my Countrymen should ever wish for the
> honour of having among them a gentry enor-
> mously wealthy, let them sell their Farms and
> pay rack'd Rents; the Scale of the Landlord
> will rise as that of the Tenants is depress'd,
> who will soon become poor, tattered, dirty, and
> abject in Spirit. Had I never been in the Amer-
> ican Colonies, but was to form my Judgment
> of Civil Society by what I have lately seen, I
> would never advise a Nation of Savages to
> admit of Civilization: For I assure you, that,
> in the Possession and Enjoyment of the various
> Comforts of Life, compar'd to these People
> every Indian is a Gentleman: And the Effect
> of this kind of Civil Society seems only to be,
> the depressing Multitudes below the Savage
> State that a few may be rais'd above it.

After reading the intercepted letters of Governor
Thomas Hutchinson of Massachusetts urging the
British Ministry to undertake harsh, repressive
measures in America, Franklin redirected his outrage: "My Resentment against this Country, for
its arbitrary Measures in governing us . . . since
my Conviction by these Papers that these Measures
were projected, advised, and called for by Men of
Character among ourselves . . . has been exceedingly
abated." Half a year later, in July, 1773, Franklin
hoped that a passing threat of war with Spain might
heal the breach. America would join Britain "in

every War she makes, to the greater Annoyance and Terror of her Enemies; [she benefits from] our Employment of her Manufactures, and Enriching of her Merchants by our Commerce. . . . On our side, we have to expect the Protection she can afford us, and the Advantage of a common Umpire in our Disputes, thereby preventing Wars we might otherwise have with each other; so that we can without Interruption go on with our Improvements, and increase our Numbers. We ask no more of her, and she should not think of forcing more from us." Franklin's vision of empire, even after eight years of what he regarded as incredibly stupid administration of colonial affairs, was still strong enough to lead him to grasp at any straw which might maintain its bonds.

Two pieces printed in London newspapers in September, 1773, show Franklin as a master satirist and reveal his outrage at the treatment accorded the colonies. In *Rules by Which a Great Empire May Be Reduced to a Small One*, Franklin paraded all the deeds and doctrines of British Ministers since 1763:

I. Consider, that a great empire, like a great cake, is most easily diminished at the edges . . . as you get rid of your remotest provinces, the next may follow in order . . . IV. However peaceably your colonies have submitted to your government . . . you are to *suppose* them always inclined to revolt . . . Quarter troops among them, who by their insolence may *provoke* the rising of mobs . . : By this means, like the husband who uses his wife ill *from suspicion*, you may in time convert your *suspicions* into *realities*. V. If you can find prodigals, who have ruined their fortunes, broken gamesters or stockjobbers, these may do well as *governors;* for they will probably be rapacious, and provoke the people by their extortions . . . IX. Remember

to make your arbitrary tax more grievous to
your provinces, by public declarations importing
that your power of taxing them has *no limits*
. . . This will probably weaken every idea of
*security in their property,* and convince them,
that under such a government they *have nothing
they can call their own* . . . XV. Convert the
brave, honest officers of your *navy* into pimping
tide-waiters and colony officers of the *customs.*
Let those, who in time of war fought gallantly
in defence of commerce . . . in peace be taught to
prey upon it . . . Thus shall the trade of your
colonists suffer more from their friends in
time of peace, than it did from their enemies
in war. Then let these boats crews land upon
every farm in their way, rob the orchards,
steal the pigs and the poultry, and insult the
inhabitants. If the injured and exasperated
farmers . . . should attack the aggressors . . .
threaten to carry all the offenders three thousand miles to be hanged, drawn, and quartered.
*O! this will work admirably!* . . . XVII. If you
see *rival nations* rejoicing at the prospect of
your disunion, and endeavouring to promote
it . . . let not that *alarm* or offend you. Why
should it, since you all mean *the same thing?*

In *An Edict by the King of Prussia,* Franklin pur-
ported to print a proclamation by Frederick the
Great extending to England, as having been settled
by emigrants from Saxony, the same measures
England had inflicted on her plantations in America. Absurdities abounded. English iron foundries
were to be closed, her trade restricted, and her hat-
makers to be put out of business; Prussian thieves
were ordered transported to England, and any
Englishmen who protested were to be returned to
Prussia for trial according to Prussian law. The
two satires were reprinted widely and were more

embarrassing to the British Ministry than hundreds of pages of political polemic or constitutional theory. Pleased, Franklin wrote his sister: "Of late . . . I have been saucy, and in two Papers . . . I have held up a Looking-Glass in which some Ministers may see their ugly Faces, and the Nation its Injustice. These Papers have been much taken Notice of, many are pleas'd with them, and a few very angry."

After Franklin's friends in Massachusetts published some letters he had told them were to be kept secret and he was forced to confess his breach of confidence, Lord North saw a chance to humble the troublesome agent. At a hearing before the Privy Council in January, 1774, Solicitor General Alexander Wedderburn abused Franklin for an hour with "invective ribaldry," and, full of arrogance, refused to receive a petition from Massachusetts. The next day Franklin was removed as postmaster general and henceforth he had no more official meetings with British ministers. Discouraged, Franklin wrote:

. . . it may be supposed, that I am very angry on this occasion . . . indeed, what I feel on my own account is half lost in what I feel for the public. When I see, that all petitions and complaints of grievances are so odious to government, that even the mere pipe which conveys them [Franklin] becomes obnoxious, I am at a loss to know how peace and union are to be maintained or restored between the different parts of the empire . . . Wise governments have . . . generally received petitions with some indulgence, even when but slightly founded. Those, who think themselves injured by their rulers, are sometimes, by a mild and prudent answer, convinced of their error. But where complaining is a crime, hope becomes despair.

News of the Boston Tea Party and other acts of violence in America alarmed Franklin and made him once again advise patience and accommodation. "The violent Destruction of the Tea seems to have united all Parties here against [Massachusetts]. . . . I cannot but hope . . . Satisfaction [is] proposed if not made; for such a Step will remove much of the Prejudice now entertain'd against us, and put us again on a fair Footing in contending for our old Privileges as Occasion may require." He felt the injustice of the Tea Party strongly enough to offer, in later negotiations, to put up bond himself to repay the owners of the cargo.

In September, 1774, news of spirited but orderly resistance in America to British measures revived Franklin's hope for a peaceful settlement. "If the Non-Consumption Agreement should become general, and be firmly adhered to, this Ministry must be ruined, and our Friends succeed them, from whom we may hope a great Constitutional Charter to be confirmed by King, Lords, and Commons, whereby our Liberties shall be recognized and established, as the only sure Foundation of that Union so necessary for our Common welfare." Brooding on the evils of disrupting the empire and the measures causing it, Franklin wrote for the last time of his imperial vision:

History affords us many instances of the ruin of states, by the prosecution of measures ill-suited to the temper and genius of their people. The ordaining of laws in favour of *one* part of the nation [empire], to the prejudice and oppression of *another,* is certainly the most erroneous and mistaken policy. An *equal* dispensation of protection, rights, privileges, and advantages, is what every part is entitled to, and ought to enjoy; it being a matter of no moment to the state, whether a subject grows rich and flourishing on the Thames or the Ohio, in Edinburgh or Dublin.

In the winter of 1774-75, seeking desperately to stave off violence and civil war, Franklin entered unofficial negotiations with Lord Chatham (William Pitt), Lord Hyde, Lord Howe, and other eminent Englishmen, but by then it was too late. Franklin declared correctly that the colonies would insist on measures granting home rule in all but the most general empire matters, and the British were bound to insist on a recognition of the complete sovereignty of Parliament. Furthermore, neither side was willing to take the blame for the depredations already committed, so the empire fell apart before Franklin's anguished eyes.

When Lord Howe tried to tempt Franklin to desert the colonies by offering him high office, and when the House of Lords ridiculed Chatham's program for conciliation, Franklin packed for home (now Pennsylvania) thoroughly disgusted:

> When I consider the extream corruption prevalent among all Orders of Men in this old rotten State, and the glorious publick Virtue so predominant in our rising Country, I cannot but apprehend more Mischief than Benefit from a closer Union. . . . Here Numberless and needless Places, enormous Salaries, Pensions, Perquisites, Bribes, groundless Quarrels, foolish Expeditions, false Accounts or no Accounts, Contracts and Jobbs, devour all Revenue, and produce continual Necessity in the Midst of natural Plenty. I apprehend, therefore, that to unite us intimately will only be to corrupt and poison us also.

Seeing little in England of the qualities extolled in *Pilgrim's Progress* or little heed paid to the pre-

cepts of *Poor Richard,* Franklin could no longer take
pride in his mother country.

Back in America, ready to declare independence
and busy preparing Pennsylvania and the united
colonies for war, Franklin exulted at the difference
between Philadelphia and London:

> Congress [has resolved] to give Britain one
> more chance, one opportunity more, of recover-
> ing the friendship of the colonies; which, how-
> ever, I think she has not sense enough to em-
> brace, and so I conclude she has lost them for
> ever.
> She has begun to burn our seaport towns . . .
> if she wishes to recover our commerce, are these
> the probable means? She must certainly be dis-
> tracted; for no tradesman out of Bedlam ever
> thought of increasing the number of his cus-
> tomers, by knocking them on the head; or of
> enabling them to pay their debts, by burning
> their houses. . . . She is now giving us such
> miserable specimens of her government, that
> we shall ever detest and avoid it, as a complica-
> tion of robbery, murder, famine, fire, and
> pestilence. . . . We have not yet applied to any
> foreign power for assistance . . . yet it is natural
> to think of it, if we are pressed. . . . [Congress
> and the Committees of Safety] proceed with
> the greatest unanimity, and their meetings are
> well attended. It will scarce be credited in Brit-
> ain, that men can be as diligent with us from
> zeal for the public good, as with you for thou-
> sands per annum. Such is the difference be-
> tween uncorrupted new states, and corrupted
> old ones.
> Great frugality and great industry are now
> become fashionable here. Gentlemen, who used
> to entertain with two or three courses, pride
> themselves now in treating with simple beef and

pudding. By these means, and the stoppage of
our consumptive trade with Britain, we shall
be better able to pay our voluntary taxes for
the support of our troops.

Thus, in signing the Declaration of Independence,
Franklin set the seal on the last chapter of his own
education, or re-education, in public philosophy.
Since hearing Increase Mather score the evil tyrant
Louis XIV and praise the glorious Protestant monarchy of Great Britain, Franklin had traveled a
long road. Nearly all the particulars of his politics
had been overturned. From ardent monarchist, he
had become an equally ardent republican. From believing the English Constitution to be the best in
the world, he had come to think it the worst. From
believing that a king and noble lords were a genuine
aristocracy, he had come to see them as decadent,
despicable thieves. From seeing France as an eternal
enemy, he had come to think of her as a potentially
invaluable friend. From Richard Burton's sense of
the divine, infallible goodness of the British royal
house, Franklin had come first to a pragmatic loyalty and then to an equally pragmatic antipathy.
But in spite of all these transformations, in helping
Jefferson draft the Declaration of Independence and
then in signing it at age seventy, Franklin was
doing no more than fulfilling the deepest commitments of his long, active life. Though he understood
and accepted the Lockean justification Jefferson
prefaced to the Declaration, Franklin's subscription
to it had the firmer foundation of a lifetime of intrepid effort to effect the common weal. In 1776
the common weal required independence from England.

As a lad in Boston, Franklin had lived in one of
the most self-conscious *common-wealths* ever devised
by man. In helping found the Massachusetts Bay
Colony, John Winthrop had observed: ". . . we must
consider that we shall be as a city upon a hill, the

eyes of all people are upon us . . . the care of the
public must oversway all private respects, by which
not only conscience, but mere civil policy doth bind
us, for it is a true rule that particular estates cannot
subsist in the ruin of the public." Though Winthrop
and his successors despised "a mere democracy" and
taught young Puritans a stern duty of obedience to
the magistrates, this obedience, as John Wise, Jonathan Mayhew, and other Puritan clergymen pointed
out, was due *only* to magistrates ruling honorably
in the public interest; otherwise disobedience to
law and obedience to conscience was required. The
Boston of Franklin's boyhood was a tightly controlled oligarchy if not a theocracy, but it was
also, especially for pious families like the Franklins,
a community of saints and brethren. Its public
philosophy was concern yourself for the welfare of
your neighbors—if they are deserving of it (which
they would be if good church members), and obey
the magistrates—if they rule with wisdom and goodness (which they would do as stewards of the Kingdom of God). Franklin subscribed to the reservations
as well as the obligations, which of course is the
same as saying that he placed conscience and virtue
above formality and blind obedience.

In Philadelphia, excited by the new, liberating
ideas he had learned from Locke, Addison, and
others, and emboldened by his own swift accomplishments, he soon enlarged his role in community
affairs. As a printer and businessman he appreciated
how freedom and private enterprise invigorated men,
but he never for a moment supposed that the fruit
of his labor and that of his neighbors was not subject
to a levy by the community for its common purposes.
But the purposes had to be *common*, that is, they
had to be genuinely in the interests of all. Though
men might dispute legitimately, as Franklin often
did, over what the public interest was or how to
seek it, there were abundant instances, sad to say,
in which that interest was clearly unheeded. In

such cases good men should protest and if necessary resist. Franklin's experience in promoting hospitals, libraries, and schools permitted him to feel in his heart, in a way scarcely possible for the mere observer or theorist, the priority of the welfare of the community. When he entered public life, he had no need to retire to his study to learn a political theory. He did not need to read Algernon Sidney to know that the feudal privileges of the proprietary family in Pennsylvania or arbitrary measures by alien ministers were unjust, any more than he needed Locke to tell him that such iniquity, persisted in, justified extreme measures of resistance —even rebellion in the absence of other recourse.

Before he left Pennsylvania, Franklin had translated the excitement of exploration and adventure learned vicariously from Richard Burton into his own grand yet down-to-earth vision of American destiny, and he had made this vision part of his sense of what the common good required. He and his friends, and thousands of others throughout the colonies, had in their own experience forged a way of life and an attitude toward their land which demanded for fulfillment relatively unfettered opportunity to develop and settle the North American continent. If one of Franklin's paths to Independence Hall on the fourth of July, 1776, came from his father's conviction setting conscience above law, another came from his own conviction, acquired in an active lifetime, that damming up the enterprise and progress of an energetic people was tyranny. The inevitable corollary to this, for the British Empire, was that so long as it opened paths for enterprise as it had done under Pitt's leadership, it would have the unflagging loyalty of men like Franklin; when it did not, it forfeited their devotion.

In England, Franklin had an opportunity to see first hand and reflect upon the real merits of the government and society of his mother country. He had no preconceived notions of what, abstractly, was "the best government," except his as yet unquestioned glorification of the British Constitution. In admiring Pitt, in coming to respect the liberal ideas of many members of Parliament, and in loving the culture and refinement he found "at home," Franklin's English pride reached new heights, but, as British ministers fatefully failed to see, without in the least diminishing his sense of common weal or his faith in a free, expanding empire. Then, between 1765 and 1775, slight, insult, stupidity, injustice, and venality one after the other drove Franklin reluctantly but relentlessly from his English patriotism. First councillors like Lord Granville put him on guard against the despotic ideas of many mighty nobles. Then jobbery in the House of Commons destroyed his faith in the virtue of that supposed bulwark of the rights of Englishmen. Next came disgust with the part George III, the good youth whose coronation Franklin had hailed in 1760, played in driving his ministers to repression and tyranny in America. Finally he saw clearly, beside the poverty of the poor and the rottenness of the rich, that society in America, despite its crudeness, was infinitely more virtuous and more prosperous than that of old England. When Franklin signed the Declaration of Independence, he in effect reassured his colleagues that they need have little fear of starting anew in the family of nations; he, a sage whose name was revered around the world and who had lived among the great of Europe for nearly two decades, was there to tell them they were right and could face the future with confidence.

Thomas Jefferson once remarked that Franklin was the only American he ever knew who had not been spoiled, or even despoiled, by living a few years in Europe. Jefferson had in mind the numerous young Americans who, dazzled by the glitter of courts and the refinement of the nobility, became ashamed of the simple, sometimes crude, life of their own country. Franklin's son William and his grandson William Temple, for example, each lived in Europe for many years and each in the long run, a stranger in America, was captured by "the courtly muses of Europe" of which Emerson was to warn. England and later France tempted Franklin himself to make his home there, but first at seventy and then at eighty, he undertook perilous ocean voyages to return to America. The older man thought he had taught his son and grandson his own principles of enterprise and independence, but they did not share his *experiences* of freedom and of progress through work. No amount of carefully guided reading or admonition could substitute for the life of action recorded in the *Autobiography*.

In becoming more rather than less staunchly independent in his old age, Franklin dramatized that a new attitude toward life had taken root in America, and that this attitude had resulted in a revolutionary public philosophy. Clothed in memorable words by Jefferson and embodied in forms of government by Madison, the attitude became a legacy of all mankind. In his life in America, Franklin had exhibited the personal qualities necessary if the words and forms were to result in an "empire of liberty" rather than in chaos. In returning to America, he told his countrymen in effect to go ahead, to have confidence that the new nation they had dared to envision would measure up to and possibly surpass the great powers of Europe. Franklin did not, as his enemies charged, conjure up independence in a fit of pique at England, nor was he even its chief spokesman or theorist. He merely gave it its character, and the confidence to come into being.

# Chapter VIII

# The Art of Congeniality

As if to prepare himself for his personal and diplomatic triumphs in France during the American Revolution, Franklin had in England ripened his capacity for intimate friendship, and practiced his way of greeting life with forbearance and tranquility if not with pleasure. He wrote in 1772, in a moment of vanity, that "nothing can be more agreeable [than my situation here] . . . a general respect paid me by the learned, a number of friends and acquaintance among them, with whom I have a pleasing intercourse; a character of so much weight, that it has protected me when some power would have done me injury . . . my company so much desired, that I seldom dine at home in winter, and could spend the whole summer in the country-houses of inviting friends, if I chose it. Learned and ingenious foreigners, that came to England, almost all make a point of visiting me; for my reputation is still higher abroad than here." Franklin's easy optimism and his calm faith in man and society, an important aspect of his habit of mind, arose in large part from his marvelous gift for friendship.

Nothing shows this better than the delight he took, when past his fiftieth birthday, in talking and writing to three charming young ladies. The first, Catharine Ray (later Greene), was twenty-four when Franklin met her in Boston in 1755 and traveled with her to Rhode Island. Her bright conversation and unaffected letters delighted him:

The small News, the domestic Occurrences among our Friends, the natural Pictures you draw of Persons, the sensible Observations and Reflections you make, and the easy chatty Manner in which you express every thing, all contribute to heighten the Pleasure [of your letters]; and the more, as they remind me of those Hours and Miles that we talk'd away so agreably, even in a Winter Journey, a wrong Road, and a soaking Shower. . . . As to your Spelling, don't let those laughing Girls put you out of Conceit with it. 'Tis the best in the world, for every Letter of it stands for something.

When Franklin heard "his Katy" had been visiting in Boston, "gay and lovely as usual," he offered, tongue in cheek, "some fatherly Advice. Kill no more Pigeons than you can eat. Be a good Girl, and don't forget your Catechism. Go constantly to Meeting—or Church—till you get a good Husband; then stay at home, and nurse the Children, and live like a Christian. Spend your spare Hours, in sober Whisk, Prayers, or learning to Cypher. You must practice *Addition* to your Husband's Estate, by Industry and Frugality; *Subtraction* of all unnecessary Expences; *Multiplication* (I would gladly have taught you that myself, but you thought it was time enough, and you wou'dn't learn) he will soon make you a Mistress of it." Less than a year before he died, Franklin wrote her that "among the felicities of my life I reckon your friendship, which I shall remember with pleasure as long as that life lasts." The letters recording the bond are among the most delightful ever written and show admirably Franklin's ability to combine sober good sense with double-edged humor, keys at once to the earnestness and to the detachment with which he viewed life.

In England, his landlady's daughter, Polly Stevenson, stimulated Franklin again to write some of his finest letters. At eighteen, she was pleased and flattered at the famous philosopher's attentiveness, and soon engaged him in scientific correspondence. In one letter he explained for her the principle of a barometer, and the way insects aided mankind. A few months later he explained why water became warm by pumping and wrote in five pages as full and clear an account of ocean tides as has ever been written, concluding:

> After writing 6 Folio Pages of Philosophy to a young Girl, is it necessary to finish such a Letter with a Compliment? Is not such a Letter of itself a Compliment? Does it not say, she has a Mind thirsty after Knowledge, and capable of receiving it; and that the most agreable things one can write to her are those that tend to the Improvement of her Understanding? It does indeed say all this, but then it is still no Compliment; it is no more than plain honest Truth, which is not the Character of a Compliment. So if I would finish my Letter in the *Mode*, I should yet add something that means nothing, and is *merely* civil and polite. But, being naturally awkward at every Circumstance of Ceremony, I shall not attempt it. I had rather conclude abruptly with what pleases me more than any Compliment can please you, that I am allow'd to subscribe myself your affectionate Friend, B. FRANKLIN.

In 1783 Franklin wrote of their friendship:

> In looking forward Twenty-five Years seems a long Period, but, in looking back, how short! Could you imagine, that 'tis now full a Quarter of a Century since we were first acquainted? It was 1757. During the greatest Part of the

Time, I lived in the same House with my dear deceased Friend, your Mother; of course you and I saw and convers'd with each other much and often. It is to all our Honours, that in all that time we never had among us the smallest Misunderstanding. Our Friendship has been all clear Sunshine, without the least Cloud in its Hemisphere. Let me conclude by saying to you, what I have had too frequent Occasions to say to my other remaining old Friends, "The fewer we become, the more let us love one another."

During Franklin's long residence in England, Polly wrote his wife about his friends and domestic arrangements, and he acted as her counselor during a courtship which resulted in her marriage to a brilliant young doctor. After Franklin returned to Philadelphia from France in 1785, crippled with gout and ten years a widower, Polly at his urging crossed the ocean to be near her old, adored friend, and, it seemed, to bring her three children (her husband had died over ten years before) to the land of opportunity which she saw behind every facet of Franklin's outlook on life. Polly Stevenson's attachment to the expansive American shows at its best the fascination the "new man of the new world" had for people of the old.

The five daughters of Bishop Jonathan Shipley, the only cleric in the House of Lords who upheld American rights, furnished Franklin with an abundance of the sprightly, charming company he enjoyed so much. He told the Bishop's wife of his conversation with her eleven-year-old daughter, Kitty, whose shyness he soon overcame during a long coach ride to London:

The first Stage we were rather pensive. I tried several Topics of Conversation, but none

of them would hold. But after Breakfast we
began to recover Spirits, and had a good deal
of Chat. Will you hear some of it? . . . don't
you wish your Sisters married? Yes. All but
Emily; I would not have her married. Why?
Because I can't spare her, I can't part with her.
The rest may marry as soon as they please, so
they do but get good Husbands. We then took
upon us to consider for 'em what sort of Husbands would be fittest for every one of them.
We began with Georgiana. She thought a
Country Gentleman, that lov'd Travelling and
would take her with him, that lov'd Books and
would hear her read to him; I added, that
had a good Estate and was a Member of Parliament and lov'd to see an Experiment now and
then. This she agreed to . . . as Emily was
very handsome we might expect an Earl for
her. So having fix'd her, as I thought, a
Countess, we went on to Anna-Maria. She,
says Kitty, should have a rich Man that has
a large Family and a great many things to
take care of; for she is very good at managing,
helps my Mama very much, can look over Bills,
and order all sorts of Family Business. . . . And
now what shall we do for Kitty? . . . I suppose
that tho' the rest have resolv'd against the
Army, she may not yet have made so rash a
Resolution. Yes, but she has: Unless, now, an
old one, an old General that has done fighting,
and is rich . . . some how or other all the old
Men take to me, all that come to our House
like me better than my other Sisters . . . He
must be an old Man of 70 or 80, and take me
when I am about 30: And then you know I
may be a rich young Widow.

"Thus," Franklin told Kitty's mother, "we chatted
on, and she was very entertaining quite to Town."
Such a man, who could master so well the intricate

task of conversing sensibly with an eleven-year-old
girl and then write of it so engagingly to her
mother, would have ideal habits for dealing with
the complexities and civilities of the court of
Versailles.

Though Franklin's wife, Deborah, did not share
importantly in his intellectual life, their relationship
was always a tender one and shows how large his
deep humanity loomed in his philosophy of life. He
tells in the *Autobiography* of the more than forty
years they spent in loving wedlock and of how
fortunate he considered himself to be in having
such a good helpmate for a wife. When he left
for England in 1757, he wrote her that "I leave
Home, and undertake this long Voyage more chear-
fully, as I can rely on your Prudence in the Management of my Affairs, and Education of my dear
Child." After nearly six months in London, Franklin wrote of how much he missed his family: " 'Tis
true, the regard and friendship I meet with from
persons of worth, and the conversation of ingenious
men, give me no small pleasure; but at this time
of life, domestic comforts afford the most solid
satisfaction, and my uneasiness at being absent
from my family, and longing desire to be with
them, make me often sigh in the midst of cheerful
company."
More revealing about Franklin's habit of mind
than these rather conventional sentiments, though,
are the humor and good-natured affection which
appear regularly in his letters to Deborah. While
attending an Indian conference on the frontier, he
wrote in disappointment and reproach at not receiving a letter from her, but without the least
hint of anger or spite:

I wrote you a few days since, by a special
messenger, . . . expecting to hear from you by
his return, . . . but he is just now returned

without a scrap for poor us. So I had a good mind not to write you by this opportunity; but I never can be ill-natured enough, even when there is the most occasion. . . . I think I won't tell you that we are well, nor that we expect to return about the middle of the week, nor will I send you a word of news; that's poz. . . . I am, Your *loving* husband, B. Franklin. P.S. I have *scratched out the loving words,* being writ in haste by mistake, when I *forgot I was angry.*

Plain, housewifely, and unsophisticated, Deborah Franklin did not belong in her husband's cultivated, drawing-room world, and she showed no inclination to join in that part of his life, but their "domestic felicity," as he put it, contributed significantly to his tranquil outlook and doubtless impressed on him countless times how important prudence and happiness in the most intimate relationships are to an evenly balanced view of mankind.

Franklin's letters to his sister Jane Mecom are full of wit and wisdom turned to homely affairs, and show further his firm, affectionate regard for his family. After sending her a few trifling presents, he wrote: "I received here your letter of extravagant thanks, which put me in mind of the Story of the Member of Parliament, who began one of his Speeches with saying, he thank'd God he was born and bred a Presbyterian, on which another took leave to observe, that the Gentleman must needs be of a most grateful Disposition, since he was thankful for such very small Matters." When Jane wrote, harassed with the care of their impoverished seventy-nine-year-old sister (Franklin furnished her a house rent-free), he replied:

As *having their own Way,* is one of the greatest Comforts of Life, to old People, I think their Friends should endeavour to accommodate them in that, as well as in any thing else. When they have long liv'd in a House, it becomes natural to them, they are almost as closely connected with it as the Tortoise with his Shell, they die if you tear them out of it. Old Folks and old Trees, if you remove them, 'tis ten to one that you kill them. So let our good old Sister be no more importun'd on that head. We are growing old fast our selves, and shall expect the same kind of Indulgencies. If we give them, we shall have a Right to receive them in our Turn. . . .

I hope you visit Sister as often as your Affairs will permit, and afford her what Assistance and Comfort you can, in her present Situation. *Old Age, Infirmities,* and *Poverty,* join'd, are Afflictions enough; the *Neglect and Slight* of Friends and near Relations, should never be added. People in her Circumstances are apt to suspect this sometimes without Cause: *Appearances* should therefore be attended to, in our Conduct towards them, as well as *Realities.*

A month later Franklin wrote her about a squabble in which Jane had asked him to favor her family over that of their brother John. After advising tactfully that energy was better spent at work than in disputes, he concluded:

. . . if my friends require of me to gratify not only their inclinations, but their resentments, they expect too much of me. Above all things I dislike family quarrels, and when they happen among my relations, nothing gives me more pain. If I were to set myself up as a judge of those subsisting between you and brother's widow and children, how unqualified must I be, at this distance, to determine rightly, especially having heard but one side. They always treated me with friendly and affectionate regard, you have done the same. What can I say between you, but that I wish you were reconciled, and that I will love that side best that is most ready to forgive and oblige the other.

In these and other letters which covered a span of over sixty years, Franklin's longest and largest surviving correspondence, the abounding humor, kindliness, and good sense mark their author as one who followed Carlyle's advice to be charitable first to those nearest at hand.

Since by 1776 much of the world had come to admire these human qualities in Franklin, when he arrived in France as a commissioner from the new United States the acclaim for his personality very nearly obscured his diplomatic mission. His procession from Nantes to Paris was triumphant, and there he was wined and dined by French literary and scientific notables. Crowds gathered in the streets to watch him pass and soon his likeness appeared on medallions, snuffboxes, rings, clocks, vases, handkerchiefs, and pocket knives. Louis XVI in a fit of jealously is said to have presented a court lady who, he thought, admired Franklin too much with a chamber pot adorned with his picture. With his sober brown coat, crab-tree walking stick, and homely bifocal spectacles, he was a picture of republican simplicity, curiously resplendent in a crowd of fashionably dressed courtiers.

Recognizing the value of this rustic pose in gaining French support and recognition for the United States, Franklin cultivated his distinctiveness, even letting people think, since it improved his "image," that he was a Quaker. He arrived in France much more than a commissioner from a struggling new republic fighting France's mortal foe. He was Poor Richard who by dint of his own energy and genius had, as Turgot said, "snatched the lightning from the sky and the sceptre from tyrants." To French philosophe opinion, he was a peerless hero, living proof of all their hopeful theories about man and society.

The love affair between Franklin and the French reached its climax at a meeting of the French Academy dryly described by John Adams:

> Voltaire and Franklin were both present, and there presently arose a general Cry that M. Voltaire and M. Franklin should be introduced to each other. This was done and they bowed and spoke to each other. This was no Satisfaction. There must be something more. Neither of our Philosophers seemed to divine what was wished or expected. . . . The Clamour continued, until the explanation came out "Il faut s'embrasser, a la françoise." The two Aged Actors upon this great Theatre of Philosophy and frivolity then embraced each other by hugging one another in their Arms and kissing each others cheeks, and then the tumult subsided. And the Cry immediately spread through the whole Kingdom and I suppose all over Europe, "Qu'il etoit charmant. Oh! il etoit enchantant, de voir Solon et Sophocle embrassants. How charming it was! Oh! It was enchanting to see Solon and Sophocles embracing!"

In becoming the real-life fulfillment of philosophe dreams, Franklin joined deed to thought, reversing the pattern of his early life where over and over again he worked toward ideas as he acted in public affairs. In France he personified the ideals and aspirations of Voltaire and the other philosophes and proved a powerful force in popularizing them all over France and Europe. While showing proper deference to the King and in no way criticizing the Old Regime, Franklin nevertheless gave a mighty boost to the liberalizing forces which led to the

French Revolution and which spread over Europe
in the nineteenth century. Ultimately feudalism and
privileged nobility fell before the irresistible example
of the Philadelphia printer.

The personal triumph inspired anew Franklin's
gift for spreading wit and charm among his friends.
When his stepniece wrote of rumors in Boston that
he flirted with French ladies, he explained:

This is the civilest Nation upon Earth. Your
first Acquaintances endeavour to find out what
you like, and they tell others. If 'tis understood
that you like Mutton, dine where you will
find Mutton. Somebody, it seems, gave it out
that I lov'd Ladies; and then every body presented me their Ladies (or the Ladies presented
themselves) to be *embrac'd,* that is to have their
Necks kiss'd. For as to kissing of Lips or
Cheeks, it is not the Mode here, the first, is
reckon'd rude, and the other may rub off the
Paint. The French Ladies have however 1000
other ways of rendering themselves agreable;
by their various Attentions and Civilities, and
their sensible Conversation. 'Tis a delightful
People to live with.

In responding to civilities and in being the sage
the French wanted him to be, Franklin wrote one
of the world's most delightful chapters in human
relations.

Among the ladies, Franklin's favorites were Mme
Brillon, brilliant, handsome, talented wife of a
rather dull treasury official, and the famed Mme
Helvetius. a rich, aging widow, herself a philosopher
of note, and renowned for her weekly dinners for the
brightest intellectuals of Paris and Versailles. Twice
a week Franklin went to Mme Brillon's for tea and
conversation, to play chess, and to hear her and
her children at their music. "People have the audac-

ity," she wrote playfully, "to criticize my pleasant
habit of sitting on your knee, and yours of always
asking me for what I always refuse." Responding
in the same mood, Franklin tried a novel approach
in seeking her favors:

> People commonly speak of *Ten* Command-
> ments. I have been taught that there are *twelve*.
> The *first* was: *Increase and Multiply* and re-
> plenish the Earth. The *twelfth* is, A new Com-
> mandment I give unto you, *that ye love one
> another*. It seems to me they are a little misplac'd,
> and that the last should have been the first.
> However, I never made any Difficulty about
> that, but was always willing to obey them both
> whenever I had an Opportunity. Pray tell me,
> my dear Casuist, whether my keeping religious-
> ly these two Commandments, tho' not in the
> Decalogue, may not be accepted in Compensation
> for my breaking so often one of the Ten,
> I mean that which forbids Coveting my Neigh-
> bor's Wife, and which I *confess* I break con-
> stantly, God forgive me, as often as I see or
> think of my lovely Confessor [Mme Brillon].
> And I am afraid I should never be able to repent
> of the Sin, even if I had the full Possession of
> her.

Only Franklin knew exactly how serious he intended this approach to be. One suspects, however, that he and Mme Brillon understood the limits
of their friendship, and at the same time played
to the full the fashionable game which required
every gallant man to seek as cleverly as possible
favors every modest woman would decline as tempt-
ingly as she could. In such sport, Franklin's nimble
mind found wide scope.

Franklin proposed marriage to Mme Helvetius,
again with a seriousness only he could know, and,
learning of her refusal, wrote her of his dream of

meeting her deceased husband in the Elysian Fields. Upon discovering that M. Helvetius, though revering his earthly wife, had taken another one in heaven, Franklin wrote Mme Helvetius of how he had explained to her husband that she had been more faithful:

. . . several good offers have been made to her, all of which she has refused. I confess to you that I myself have loved her to the point of distraction, but she was hard-hearted to my regard, and has absolutely rejected me for love of you. I pity you, he said, for your bad fortune; for truly she is a good and beautiful woman and very loveable.

Then, Franklin wrote,

the new Madame H—— entered . . . at which instant I recognized her to be Madame F——, my old American friend [wife]. I reclaimed to her. But she told me coldly, "I have been your good wife for forty-nine years and four months, nearly a half century; be content with that. Here I have formed a new connection, which will endure to eternity."

Offended by this refusal of my Eurydice, I suddenly decided to leave these ungrateful spirits, to return to the good earth, to see again the sunshine and you. Here I am! Let us revenge ourselves.

In these exchanges, and in *Dialogue Between Franklin and the Gout, The Whistle, The Morals of Chess,* and other bagatelles which Franklin printed on his private press in France to amuse and edify his friends, we see not only a part of his mind and imagination which attention to his more serious writings might miss, but a revelation of the *way* his mind worked when considering more weighty topics. It showed, as Carl Becker has said, Franklin's "disposition to take life with infinite zest and yet with humorous detachment." His intense enjoyment of French society and the unique role he played in it never *engaged* him, never prevented him from having an eye for its foibles or an ear for its discords and minor keys. His devotion to Mmes Brillon and Helvetius was unreserved and he may have sought more than they in propriety could yield, but he contained his admiration and desire with playful goodwill. The letters on the two additional commandments and on the meeting in the Elysian Fields in a way laugh at the writer's aspirations. He knew well that learning to laugh at oneself was an impregnable refuge of tranquillity and sanity.

Franklin was not chosen to draft the Declaration of Independence, legend has it, for fear he might conceal a joke in it. It may have been wise to entrust the more serious Jefferson with that historic document. Franklin's ability to combine earnest friendship with humorous detachment, however, enhanced his capacity to serve in public life at times when men utterly serious and involved succeeded only in fraying each other's nerves. It made perfectly good sense to him to carry into politics and diplomacy ways and habits which made him a supremely agreeable companion. A mind which could charm a sheltered Catharine Ray as easily as a sophisticated Mme Helvetius would have a great advantage in contending with the subtleties and vexations of a difficult diplomatic assignment.

# Chapter IX

# International Relations

FRANKLIN SOON DISCOVERED he would need his subtle and genial skills in abundance to fulfill his mission in France. Surrounded by suspicions and crosscurrents, he had to bring a republic taught recently to despise kings and long schooled in hatred for France into alliance with a French monarch who abhorred republicanism. Had he been perfectly direct and outspoken he would, though asking for money and support, have reproached Louis XVI for his tyranny, and he would have told his countrymen to shun the aid of a Catholic despot. The approach to France could neither have been begun nor consummated. Understanding his complex objective, however, Franklin had to show both sides the benefit of alliance. He was detached enough from doctrinaire republicanism (apostasy, his enemies charged) to see the advantage in a humble, even flattering approach to the court of Versailles, and he was good-humored enough to see that his countrymen were not as untainted by vanity and frivolity (treason, his enemies said) as they sometimes proclaimed. Franklin brought highly valuable personal traits to the weighty matters of war and diplomacy he managed in France for more than eight years.

In crossing the ocean as the agent of an independent country, Franklin, of course, had to abandon the vision of British imperial greatness which had inspired him for twenty-five years. He had

instead to devise a new formula consistent with the
realities of world power politics which would nevertheless permit renewed progress toward the persist-
ing vision of an empire of liberty, now to be sought
outside the British realm. The new United States,
though potentially invincible in Franklin's view,
were in 1776 pitifully weak and exposed to the
selfishness of international politics. Most Americans
with any knowledge of world affairs understood
perfectly that Great Britain could not be beaten
without the aid of friendly foreign powers, particularly France, which, though corrupt and nearly
bankrupt, was still Europe's grandest nation and
Britain's mortal foe. The problem, a perennial one
for new nations founded upon high-sounding declarations, was to get the vital support from the real
world without at the same time being contaminated
by those realities.

Franklin's method was as effective as it was devious. He understood that the French foreign minister,
Vergennes, could not recognize American independence immediately, so he did not demand what
he knew could not be granted, permitted Vergennes
to intrigue at court and pull diplomatic strings, and
himself accepted the adoration of the French public,
which he knew in the long run would count for more
than nagging letters to the Ministry. He helped
concoct a fictitious merchant firm to funnel French
aid to America and ingratiated himself with great
noble families such as those of the Marquis and
Marquise de Lafayette. For a year he seemed to
make no headway at all, but when news of the
victory at Saratoga (October, 1777) showed Louis
XVI that the American rebels could be taken seriously, Franklin was in a position swiftly to conclude
the vital alliance. Though the common interest of
France and the United States in humbling Great
Britain was the essential basis for the alliance,
Franklin's skill and finesse anticipated and smoothed
many obstacles along the way. Furthermore, in an

age of personal diplomacy, his international prestige and fame, unmatched by any other American, were supremely important.

In dealing so shrewdly with France, Franklin earned the suspicion and then the enmity of Americans who could not grasp the complexities he faced. Arthur Lee, an American diplomat whom Franklin later called "the most malicious Enemy I ever had," thought the fictitious merchant scheme an effort to defraud America, Franklin's patience mere idleness, and his deference to Vergennes a humiliating betrayal of American interests. To Lee the homage paid Franklin and his obvious delight in it were proof that he had been seduced by the crafty French. Though John Adams was much less paranoid than Lee and knew French aid was vital, Franklin's apparent lack of candor, order, and earnestness irritated and appalled him. Adams thought he had to rescue American honor and policy from Franklin's careless, cynical grasp. To the earnest New Englander, an American minister who held French ladies on his knee and who fawned before French officers of state ill-served the virtuous cause of the new republic. Franklin had, Adams recorded in his diary:

. . . a Passion for Reputation and Fame, as strong as you can imagine, and his Time and Thoughts are chiefly employed to obtain it, and to set Tongues and Pens male and female, to celebrating him. . . . He has the most affectionate and insinuating Way of charming the Woman or the Man that he fixes on. It is the most silly and ridiculous Way imaginable, in the Sight of an American, but it succeeds, to admiration, fullsome and sickish as it is, in Europe.

On the other hand, Franklin's successor in France, Thomas Jefferson, defended him:

He possessed the confidence of [the French] government in the highest degree, insomuch, that it may truly be said, that they were more under his influence, than he under theirs. The fact is, that his temper was so amiable and conciliatory, his conduct so rational, never urging impossibilities, or even things unreasonably inconvenient to them, in short, so moderate and attentive to their difficulties, as well as our own, that what his enemies called subserviency, I saw was only that reasonable disposition, which, sensible that advantages are not all to be on one side, yielding what is just and liberal, is the more certain of obtaining liberality and justice. Mutual confidence produces, of course, mutual confidence, and this was all which subsisted between Dr. Franklin and the government of France.

The disputes among Americans in Paris reflected differing responses to independence as well as personal antagonisms. Arthur Lee, a staunch patriot, diligent and punctual in his work, and utterly honest, was at the same time uneasy and insecure without his English nationality, and saw nothing but snares and pitfalls at the courts of Europe. John Adams was perfectly content to be merely an American and though he responded warmly to much of French culture, his deep sense that New England virtue would be seduced by more than the most guarded, formal contact with Europe, and his conviction that to be truly independent America must win her own battles, made him overly suspicious. He believed everyone in Europe stood ready, dagger in hand, to fall upon the United States at the earliest opportunity. To Lee and Adams, and to many other pure-minded patriots, plain American republicanism was enough; the break with England had in their view purged the United States of her corrupt influence and nothing could be gained from any but strictly commercial connections with the even more depraved, despotic nations on the European continent.

Franklin, on the other hand, was at home at once in France and had no need to be suspicious of her people or culture. His previous joy in English civilization and learning, in part alienated by the Declaration of Independence, could be replaced only by a corresponding delight in some other cultivated society. By 1776 Franklin was far too much a part of the universal brotherhood of the Enlightenment to be content with a parochial view of American nationhood. He welcomed close cooperation with France at a time, as Carl Van Doren has said, "when many Americans were still suspicious of their ancient foes as Catholic, despotic and immoral." Culturally and psychologically, he and other cosmopolitan Americans needed a tie with a great nation to replace the connection which they felt England had betrayed and forfeited by her oppression.

Thus Franklin was prepared to trust France, to find in her a real friend, and to welcome all the manifold associations with her that would keep America in the mainstream of Western civilization. Proud of America and convinced as he was of her great future, he never for a moment thought she could "go it alone" or supposed that she could reach her destined place in the world by disdaining all contact with it. Thus he was prepared to negotiate candidly and effectively with Vergennes without fear that he would be corrupted or would unwittingly betray American interests. Franklin's long experience of cordial human relations and his standing in the international community of science and learning permitted him to approach France warmly as a friend who might help in a mutually advantageous enterprise, rather than as a treacherous, alien enigma to be threatened or frightened temporarily and unwillingly into aiding a cause she at heart hated.

In defending France and using all his art to
secure her aid through retaining her goodwill,
Franklin became a symbol in the first great debate
of American national politics. Those who sympa-
thized with Arthur Lee and later with John Adams,
led in Congress by Richard Henry Lee and Samuel
Adams, reflected eternal suspicion of France and
generally envisioned the United States as a loose
confederation little concerned with affairs outside
the narrow boundaries of each separate state. They
were satisfied with the ancient dream of the small
republic, idyllic and pastoral, immune to the siren
calls of dynastic ambition, commerce, and luxury.
Those who welcomed Franklin's dispatches and
counsel, however, saw France as America's indispensable sponsor in the international community.
They envisioned the United States as a unified country ready to exert a beneficent power in the world,
trading with other nations, and with them bending
every effort to enhance the material and moral well-
being of mankind. As he had experienced often before, Franklin found himself supported by energetic young men, in this case including James Madison and Alexander Hamilton, who saw the strength
derived from union and who looked to the future
rather than to the past for their inspiration.

In France, as at Albany in 1754 and at Philadelphia in 1776 and 1787, Franklin had the buoyancy
and courage to hope that the power of men united
in a common enterprise could be useful to humanity.
He had no use for men of little faith who shrank
from doing anything for fear duplicity or depravity
would capture the effort. Because he felt his country strong and its people possessed of the wisdom
and courage which those who manage their own
destinies develop, he thought her more than a match
for the craft and wiles of Europe, and that she, not
the nations of the old world, was destined to lead
the way in centuries to come. The faith he had
expressed in his own prospects for a bright future

when he left Boston at age seventeen, and the faith
in the future of North America he had expressed in
*Observations Concerning the Increase of Mankind*
in 1751, had their natural extension in his confidence that after declaring independence, the United
States would, in accord with any powers of the
world that could be persuaded to help for whatever
reason, move invincibly toward extending the empire of liberty. The rest of the world, not America,
would find its ways and principles undermined and
transformed.

In fact, Franklin's view of international relations rested on the fond hope of his age that reason
would soon purge the world of war and tyranny.
Of trade he wrote:

> . . . in general I would only observe that com-
> merce, consisting in a mutual exchange of the
> necessities and conveniences of life, the more
> free and unrestrained it is, the more it
> flourishes; and the happier are all the na-
> tions concerned in it. Most of the restraints
> put upon it in different countries seem to have
> been the projects of particulars for their private
> interest, under pretence of public good. . . .
> I have seen so much Embarrassment and so
> little Advantage in all the Restraining and
> Compulsive Systems, that I feel myself strong-
> ly inclin'd to believe, that a State, which leaves
> all her Ports open to all the World upon equal
> Terms, will, by that means, have foreign Com-
> modities cheaper, sell its own Productions
> dearer, and be on the whole the most prosperous.

Franklin, like many other Americans and Europeans, had learned by experience the theory of
free trade which Adam Smith set forth in 1776
in *The Wealth of Nations*. This doctrine, supposing
that peace and prosperity would result as if guided

by an invisible hand if only individuals and nations were allowed to work and to trade freely as they thought their self-interest required, was most attractive to Franklin and others who delighted to find the affairs of men responding to the same kind of marvelously harmonious laws Isaac Newton had propounded in physics and astronomy.

To his belief in the benefits of free trade, Franklin added a faith that men at their best, in societies where virtue and justice were encouraged, could banish the scourge of war. During the American Revolution he wrote indignantly to an English friend: "You have lost by this mad War, and the Barbarity with which it has been carried on, not only the Government and Commerce of America, and the public Revenues and private Wealth arising from that Commerce, but what is more, you have lost the Esteem, Respect, Friendship, and Affection of all that great and growing People, who consider you at present, and whose Posterity will consider you, as the worst and wickedest Nation upon Earth." War in an unjust cause, Franklin added, "is nothing less than Murder." After signing the peace treaty of 1783, Franklin rejoiced "in the PEACE God has blest us with, and in the Prosperity it gives us prospect of . . . We are now Friends with England and with all Mankind. May we never see another War! for in my opinion *there never was a good War, or a bad Peace.*" The United States, Franklin thought, was destined to be an especially peaceful nation:

> Americans are Cultivators of Land; those engag'd in Fishery and Commerce are a small Number, compar'd with the Body of the People. They have ever conducted their several Governments with Wisdom, avoiding Wars and vain, expensive Projects, delighting only in their peaceable Occupations, which must, considering the Extent of their yet uncultivated

Territory, find them Employment still for Ages.
Whereas England . . . is half her Time engag'd
in some War . . . [and] is now [1777] acting
like a mad Shop-keeper, who should attempt, by
beating those that pass his Door, to make them
come in and be his Customers. . . . America, on
the other Hand, aims only at establishing her
Liberty, and that Freedom of Commerce which
will be advantageous to all Europe.

Though the Revolutionary War confirmed Franklin's lifelong belief that war as a national policy
was mad and wrong, he always supported resistance
to injustice and aggression, with force if necessary.
In 1756, impatient with Quaker pacifism and inept
negotiations by Crown agents while Indian attacks
continued in the frontier, he wrote that "I do not
believe we shall ever have a firm Peace with the
Indians till we have well drubb'd them." In 1780, as
British armies fought triumphantly through the
Carolinas and when to many it seemed necessary to
trade American rights to navigate the Mississippi
for Spanish support against England, Franklin opposed any such surrender:

I am confident that [Spain] will be wiser
than to take advantage of our Distress, and
insist on our making Sacrifices . . . the very
Proposition can only give disquiet at Present.
Poor as we are, yet, as I know we shall be rich,
I would rather agree with them to buy at a
great Price the whole of their Right on the
Mississippi, than sell a Drop of its Waters.
A Neighbour might as well ask me to sell my
Street Door.

Franklin countenanced some internal violence in
France in 1789 with the same hope he had indulged
for America in 1776. Learning of the riots of Bas-
tille Day, he wrote an English friend that "the

Convulsions in France are attended with some disagreable Circumstances; but if by the Struggle she obtains and secures for the Nation its future Liberty, and a good Constitution, a few Years' Engagement of those Blessings will amply repair all the Damages their Acquisition may have occasioned. God grant, that not only the Love of Liberty, but a thorough Knowledge of the Rights of Man, may pervade all the Nations of the Earth, so that a Philosopher may set his Foot anywhere on its Surface, and say, 'This is my Country.' " Franklin wrote in 1755 that "Those who would give up essential Liberty, to purchase a little temporary Safety, deserve neither Liberty nor Safety." He persisted in this tough-minded view, espoused in the twentieth century most eloquently by Winston Churchill, as long as he lived.

Thus, in seeking peace, believing in its benefits, and hoping for its establishment in freedom around the world, Franklin nevertheless understood international relations realistically. He had little use for the pious hope that once the American Revolutionary War was over the United States would be able to ignore the French alliance:

It is our firm connection with France, that gives us weight with England, and respect throughout Europe. If we were to break our faith with this nation, *on whatever pretence*, England would again trample us, and every other nation despise us. . . . Britain has not yet well digested the loss of its dominion over us, and has still at times some flattering hopes of recovering it. Accidents may increase those hopes, and encourage dangerous attempts . . . the true political interest of America consists in observing and fulfilling, with the greatest exactitude, the engagements of our alliance with France, and behaving at the same time towards England, so as not entirely to extinguish her hopes of a reconciliation.

Franklin understood that as a weak nation, the new United States could not stand apart from world power politics, that she would need skill and dexterity to balance French and English ambitions, and that she would have to purchase independence by persuading other nations that she sought peace, would honor her commitments, and would trade to the mutual advantage of all nations.

Franklin's hope for lasting friendship between the former colonies and the mother country rested on his effort to secure peace terms which would remove potential sources of dispute between them. He explained that "if it was meant to keep America in *danger* (as by retaining [in English hands] garrisoned places . . . and the like) . . . the consequence would be wars, and hatred." One of the English negotiators of the Peace of 1783 reported that Franklin wished for reconciliation to keep America "out of all wars. For if England disarms herself America need not fear England, and not fearing England she need not cultivate France; and as a lover of Mankind," the negotiator continued, Franklin was "happy in thinking that when England and France lose this motive for war, *their* wars also may be less frequent."*

Franklin saw that the peace and security of his country depended on reducing tensions and removing causes of conflict all over the world. As he prepared to come home from France, he summarized his hopes and advice for his country:

A few years of Peace, will improve, will restore and encrease our strength; but our future safety will depend on our union and our virtue. Britain will be long watching for ad-

---

* Quoted in Gerald Stourzh, *Benjamin Franklin and American Foreign Policy* (Chicago, 1954), p. 213. Students interested further in Franklin's theory and practice of international relations should consult this excellent book.

vantages, to recover what she has lost. If we do not convince the world, that we are a Nation to be depended on for fidelity in Treaties; if we appear negligent in paying our Debts, and ungrateful to those who have served and befriended us; our reputation, and all the strength it is capable of procuring, will be lost, and fresh attacks upon us will be encouraged and promoted by better prospects of success. Let us therefore beware of being lulled into a dangerous security; and of being both enervated and impoverished by luxury; of being weakened by internal contentions and divisions; of being shamefully extravagant in contracting private debts, while we are backward in discharging honorably those of the public; of neglect in military exercises and discipline, and in providing stores of arms and munitions of war, to be ready on occasion; for all these are circumstances that give confidence to enemies, and diffidence to friends; and the expences required to prevent a war are much lighter than those that will, if not prevented, be absolutely necessary to maintain it.

Franklin's fundamental faith was that freedom, peace, and goodwill would prevail ultimately provided only that men who valued them be willing to work and if necessary to fight for their preservation. As a realist and as an activist, he believed that good men had to act to prevent the triumph of evil. A half century of experience with British mercantilism convinced him that the tribute it exacted on commerce and the damper it put on enterprise were not worth its little advantages for a few favored national interests. Mercantilism penalized the imposer and the imposed upon by upsetting the harmonious laws which, like those governing the heavens, guided trade when it was left free. Similarly, peace benefited all nations alike, those bent on ex-

pansion and progress as well as old, stable ones.
Furthermore, virtue in foreign relations afforded
the best security. Nations that were honest, coura-
geous, and benevolent in dealing with others would be
safer at home and more able to pursue their interests
abroad. In sharing the enthusiasm for reason and
harmony which was the mark of his age, Franklin
helped fasten on American foreign policy a tradition which finds expression today, for example, in
the support of the United Nations, the strengthening
of which, one feels sure, Franklin would heartily
approve.

At the same time, though, Franklin sought to
ground his understanding of world politics in reality
and experience. An empire dedicated to dynastic
ambition or hostile aggression he thought beneath
contempt, but one which spread trade and civilization, which grew because of its manifest merits, and
which extended rather than restricted freedom, had
his wholehearted support. An empire, in other words,
which served human needs and aspirations because
it depended on such natural forces as an expanding
population or productive efficiency was in his mind
an agency of reason. He recognized, however, that
intrigues, passions, and ambitions had great power
in the world and had to be opposed steadfastly if
they were not to overwhelm the forces of virtue. He
would have refused to take sides in the debate between the "idealists" and "realists" in foreign policy.
He thought himself to be, and in fact was, utterly
realistic in dealing with foreign powers. Convinced
of England's hostility to the United States, he was
ever on guard against her ill will. His gratitude to
France and his respect for her foreign minister did
not prevent him from working behind Vergennes'
back (though not against his interests) at a vital
stage (for America) in the peace negotiations with
England.

On the other hand, his belief in the real advantages of promoting idealism in the world preserved

him from the cynical, corrupting attitude which has characterized supposed "realists" from Thrasymachus to Machiavelli and Stalin. Franklin stands in the great tradition of those who have insisted that the pursuit of virtue is practical if men value it enough to defend it with the sword as well as with words. Though some of Franklin's easy optimism that peace and freedom would triumph inevitably sounds rather hollow today, his refusal to surrender to despair in the face of grim reality teaches a timeless lesson for men who would project their goodwill to international relations.

## Chapter X

# Religion

WHEN FRANKLIN RETURNED to America in 1785, in
his eightieth year, he was, perhaps, the most famous
man in the world, known to millions in many lands,
and to his own country a founding father and its
authentic sage. He had accomplished miracles and
dined with kings, yet he retained the common touch.
He embodied an age and had stamped a nation with
his character. He was, therefore, able to speak as
from on high on any subject he chose. To emphasize
the close connection between the life he had led and
the precepts in which he believed, he wrote the
final sections of his autobiography, trying, he said,
to show others the secrets of his success. He accepted the presidency of Pennsylvania to help heal
deep wounds left by revolutionary ardor, spoke out
against Negro slavery and corruption in high office, renewed his argument for instruction in the
English language at the University of Pennsylvania,
and gave new life and dignity to the American
Philosophical Society. It seemed as though he had
been granted five years before his death to come
home and show his countrymen how useful wisdom
could be.

As becomes a sage, Franklin found occasion in his
last years to reflect on religion and politics. Throughout his life he had shown an interest in religious
questions, and his religion, or alleged lack of it,
had been discussed often by friend and foe alike. An

age which ordinarily saw a close connection between religion and conduct took a special interest in the faith of one whose life had been as remarkable as Franklin's. As he approached death, too, questions of eternity seemed to increase in relevance. Furthermore, with an experience in public affairs far exceeding that of any of his compatriots, and with the country approaching the culmination of its own nation-building efforts, a last testament from Franklin on politics seemed especially urgent. It seemed providential that canny Poor Richard, who had devoted over thirty years, with remarkable success, to the most vexing political questions in three countries, should appear in Philadelphia on the eve of the Constitutional Convention. Thus Franklin came to the end of his days as he might have wished: speaking out of the wisdom of his life to mankind on the two perennial matters which most concern and vex it. He summarized a lifetime of interest in religion with a valedictory statement of his faith in the month before he died, and he capped his public service with a valedictory performance at the Constitutional Convention of 1787.

Franklin's basic debt to his Puritan background and his own intellectual conversion to deism have been discussed (Chapter III). When under the influence of skeptical writings, Franklin had written and published in London in 1725 *A Dissertation on Liberty and Necessity*, which "from the attributes of God, his infinite wisdom, goodness and power, concluded that nothing could possibly be wrong in the world, and that vice and virtue were empty distinctions, no such things existing." In the first part of his autobiography (written in 1771), Franklin observed that the pamphlet "appear'd now not so clever a Performance as I once thought it: and I doubted whether some Error had not insinuated itself unperceiv'd into my Argument, so as to infect all that follow'd, as is common in

metaphysical Reasonings." Dissatisfied with the
deductive method of the pamphlet, Franklin tried
instead to *induce* some generalizations from his observation of life: "I grew convinc'd that *Truth, Sincerity* and *Integrity* in Dealings between Man and
Man, were of the utmost Importance to the Felicity
of Life . . . Revelation had indeed no weight with me
as such; but I entertain'd an Opinion, that tho'
certain Actions might not be bad *because* they were
forbidden by it, or good *because* it commanded them;
yet probably these Actions might be forbidden *because* they were bad for us, or commanded *because*
they were beneficial to us, in their own Natures, all
the Circumstances of things considered."

In a paper prepared for discussion by the Junto
in 1732, Franklin concluded a clever analysis of the
difficulty evil presented to the traditional argument
that God was all-good, all-wise, and all-powerful,
by observing that by "believing [in] a Providence
we have the Foundation of all true Religion; for
we should love and revere that Deity for his Goodness and thank him for his Benefits; we should
adore him for his Wisdom, fear him for his Power;
and pray to him for his Favour and Protection; and
this Religion will be a Powerful Regulator of our
Actions, give us Peace and Tranquility within our
own Minds, and render us Benevolent, Useful and
Beneficial to others."

To better guide his own religious practice after
he had become disgusted with the preaching of the
Calvinist minister in Philadelphia, Franklin drew up
some *Articles of Belief and Acts of Religion*, including a liturgy, prayers of petition and praise, and
Milton's "Hymn to the Creator" from *Paradise
Lost*. Franklin's "First Principles" began with a
belief that "there is one Supreme most perfect
Being, Author and Father of the Gods themselves,"
and that "since there is in all Men something like a
natural Principle which enclines them to DEVOTION

or the Worship of some unseen Power; . . . Therefore I think it seems required of me, and my Duty,
as a Man, to pay Divine Regards to SOMETHING."
After conceding that there may be many gods in
the universe, Franklin declared that "It is that
particular wise and good God, who is the Author and
Owner of our System, that I propose for the Object
of my Praise and Adoration," and that

> Next to the Praise due, to his Wisdom, I be-
> lieve he is pleased and delights in the Happiness
> of those he has created; and since without Vir-
> tue Man can have no Happiness in this World,
> I firmly believe he delights to see me Virtuous,
> because he is pleas'd when he sees me Happy.
>     And since he has created many Things which
> seem purely design'd for the Delight of Man,
> I believe he is not offended when he sees his
> Children solace themselves in any manner of
> pleasant Exercises and innocent Delights, and
> I think no Pleasure innocent that is to Man
> hurtful.

Reflecting on the need for virtuous people to act
in concert, and on the agreement of nearly all religions of his day on some important propositions,
Franklin summarized his own beliefs and at the
same time set down a creed which he supposed could
be the basis for a "United Party of Virtue":

That there is one God who made all things.
That he governs the World by his Providence.
That he ought to be worshiped by Adoration, Prayer
    and Thanksgiving.
But that the most acceptable Service of God is doing
    Good to Man.
That the Soul is immortal.
And that God will certainly reward Virtue and
    punish Vice either here or hereafter.

Franklin, then, rejected his father's theology, became impatient with all the intricate arguments used for and against it, and adopted for himself a deistic creed having as its foundations the inclination of man to worship a superior being, the harmony of the universe, and the need to encourage virtue in the world. In so doing, Franklin followed a pattern common among men of his day who considered themselves enlightened. Because he found his creed agreed with the "essentials" of all the religions practiced in Pennsylvania, Franklin

. . . respected them all, tho' with different degrees of Respect as I found them more or less mix'd with other Articles which without any Tendency to inspire, promote or confirm Morality, serv'd principally to divide us and make us unfriendly to one another. This Respect to all, with an Opinion that the worst had some good Effects, induc'd me to avoid all Discourse that might tend to lessen the good Opinion another might have of his own Religion; and as our Province increas'd in People, and new Places of worship were continually wanted, and generally erected by voluntary Contribution, my Mite for such purpose, whatever might be the Sect, was never refused.

Tho' I seldom attended any Public Worship, I had still an Opinion of its Propriety, and of its Utility when rightly conducted, and I regularly paid my annual Subscription for the Support of the only Presbyterian Minister or Meeting we had in Philadelphia. He us'd to visit me sometimes as a Friend, and admonish me to attend his Administrations, and I was now and then prevail'd on to do so, once for five Sundays successively. Had he been, *in my Opinion*, a good Preacher perhaps I might have continued, notwithstanding the occasion I had for the Sunday's Leisure in my Course of

Study: But his Discourses were chiefly either
polemic Arguments, or Explications of the
peculiar Doctrines of our Sect, and were all
to me very dry, uninteresting and unedify-
ing, since not a single moral Principle was inculcated or enforc'd, their Aim seeming to be
rather to make us Presbyterians than good
Citizens.

Franklin's interest in the moral benefits of religion led to a long, intimate friendship with the
famous evangelist George Whitefield, who preached
often in Philadelphia during the 1740's. Of one of
his preaching missions Franklin wrote that "it was
wonderful to see the Change soon made in the Manners of our Inhabitants; from being thoughtless or
indifferent about Religion, it seem'd as if all the
World were growing Religious; so that one could
not walk thro' the Town in an Evening without
Hearing Psalms sung in different Families of
every Street." Franklin helped collect money to
build a tabernacle for Whitefield to preach in,
printed his journals, and entertained him when he
was in Philadelphia. Though fascinated by Whitefield's magnificent voice, by his unrivaled talent for
fund-raising, and by his honest, exuberant way,
Franklin was most impressed by Whitefield's ability
to change people's conduct.

Franklin had come to his own standards of be-
havior by the habits formed in him as a child and
by reason. For the vast numbers of people less
favored by birth or less inclined to study and reason
for themselves, preaching like Whitefield's provided,
it seemed to Franklin, the best way to achieve
widespread moral improvement. To one concerned
for a city's welfare and engaged in sometimes dis-
couraging efforts to promote it, the transformation
accomplished by Whitefield's missions must have
seemed miraculous. If, as Franklin believed, the
only fundamental reform was that made in the

hearts and minds of individuals, then Whitefield's gift for causing such reformations was of incalculable benefit to mankind. "He us'd indeed sometimes to pray for my Conversion," Franklin wrote, "but never had the Satisfaction of believing that his Prayers were heard. Ours was a mere civil Friendship, sincere on both Sides, and lasted to his Death." Franklin neither agreed with Whitefield's theology nor fell under the spell of his matchless oratory, but the two men, in Franklin's view, shared a *civil* conviction, that is, that the welfare of the community in general required a faithful and upright citizenry.

To a minister who, unlike Whitefield, could not abide an easy tolerance of unorthodoxies, Franklin set forth his own religion of good works and his hope that Christians would emphasize them more:

> For my own Part, when I am employed in serving others, I do not look upon my self as conferring Favours, but as paying Debts. In my Travels and since my Settlement I have received much Kindness from Men, to whom I shall never have any Opportunity of making the least direct Return. And numberless Mercies from God, who is infinitely above being benefited by our Services. These Kindnesses from Men I can therefore only return on their Fellow-Men; and I can only show my Gratitude for those Mercies from God, by a Readiness to help his other Children and my Brethren. For I do not think that Thanks, and Compliments, tho' repeated Weekly, can discharge our real Obligations to each other, and much less those to our Creator.
> You will see in this my Notion of Good Works, that I am far from expecting (as you suppose) that I shall merit Heaven by them. By Heaven we understand, a State of Happi-

ness, infinite in Degree, and eternal in Duration: I can do nothing to deserve such Reward:
He that for giving a Draught of Water to a
thirsty Person should expect to be paid with a
good Plantation, would be modest in his De-
mands, compar'd with those who think they
deserve Heaven for the little Good they do on
Earth. Even the mix'd imperfect Pleasures we
enjoy in this World are rather from God's
Goodness than our Merit; how much more such
Happiness of Heaven. For my own part, I have
not the Vanity to think I deserve it, the Folly
to expect it, nor the Ambition to desire it; but
content myself in submitting to the Will and
Disposal of that God who made me, who has
hitherto preserv'd and bless'd me, and in whose
fatherly Goodness I may well confide, that he
will never make me miserable, and that even the
Afflictions I may at any time suffer shall tend
to my Benefit.

The Faith you mention has doubtless its use
in the World; I do not desire to see it diminished,
nor would I endeavour to lessen it in any Man.
But I wish it were more productive of Good
Works than I have generally seen it: I mean real
good Works, Works of Kindness, Charity, Mercy,
and Publick Spirit; not Holiday-keeping, Ser-
mon-Reading or Hearing, performing Church
Ceremonies, or making long Prayers, fill'd
with Flatteries and Compliments, despis'd even
by wise Men, and much less capable of pleasing
the Deity. The Worship of God is a Duty, the
hearing and reading of Sermons may be useful; but if Men rest in Hearing and Praying,
as too many do, it is as if a Tree should value
itself on being water'd and putting forth Leaves,
tho' it never produc'd any Fruit.

Your great Master tho't much less of these outward Appearances and Professions than many
of his modern Disciples. He prefer'd the Doers

of the Word to the meer Hearers; the Son that
seemingly refus'd to obey his Father and yet
perform'd his Commands, to him that profess'd
his Readiness but neglected the Works; the
heretical but charitable Samaritan, to the un-
charitable tho' orthodox Priest and sanctified
Levite: and those who gave Food to the hungry,
Drink to the Thirsty, Raiment to the Naked,
Entertainment to the Stranger, and Relief to
the Sick, &c. tho' they never heard of his
Name, he declares shall in the last Day be
accepted, when those who cry Lord, Lord; who
value themselves on their Faith tho' great
enough to perform Miracles but have neglected
good Works shall be rejected. He profess'd that
he came not to call the Righteous but Sinners to
repentance; which imply'd his modest Opinion
that there were some in his Time so good that
they need not hear even him for Improvement;
but now a days we have scarce a little Parson,
that does not think it the Duty of every Man
within his Reach to sit under his petty Ministra-
tions, and that whoever omits them offends God.
I wish to such more Humility, and to you
Health and Happiness, being Your Friend
and Servant B FRANKLIN

In response to a request for an opinion about
publishing an antireligious work, Franklin set down
his pragmatic attitude toward disbelief:

You yourself may find it easy to live a virtuous Life without the Assistance afforded by
Religion; you having a clear Perception of the
Advantages of Virtue and the Disadvantages
of Vice, and possessing a Strength of Resolution sufficient to enable you to resist common
Temptations. But think how great a Proportion of Mankind consists of weak and ignorant
Men and Women, and of inexperienc'd and in-

considerate Youth of both Sexes, who have need of the Motives of Religion to restrain them from Vice, to support their Virtue, and retain them in the Practice of it till it becomes *habitual,* which is the great Point for its Security; and perhaps you are indebted to her originally that is to your Religious Education, for the Habits of Virtue upon which you now justly value yourself. . . . Among us, it is not necessary, as among the Hottentots, that a Youth to be receiv'd into the Company of Men, should prove his Manhood by beating his Mother. I would advise you therefore not to attempt unchaining the Tyger, but to burn this Piece before it is seen by any other Person, whereby you will save yourself a great deal of Mortification from the Enemies it may raise against you, and perhaps a good deal of Regret and Repentance. If Men are so wicked as we now see them *with Religion* what would they be if *without it?*

Shortly before expressing this critique of those who undermined religious faith, Franklin had written what became a famous plea for religious toleration, a principle to which he gave lifelong and wholehearted support. He wrote, imitating the style and cadence of the King James Bible, a "new chapter" of the Book of Genesis telling "A Parable Against Persecution":

1. And it came to pass after these Things, that Abraham sat in the Door of his Tent, about the going down of the Sun.

2. And behold a Man, bowed with Age, came from the Way of the Wilderness, leaning on a Staff.

3. And Abraham arose and met him, and said unto him, Turn in, I pray thee, and wash thy

Feet, and tarry all Night, and thou shalt arise early on the Morrow, and go on thy Way.

4. And the Man said, Nay, for I will abide under this Tree.

5. But Abraham pressed him greatly; so he turned, and they went into the Tent; and Abraham baked unleavend Bread, and they did eat.

6. And when Abraham saw that the Man blessed not God, he said unto him, Wherefore dost thou not worship the most high God, Creator of Heaven and Earth?

7. And the Man answered and said, I do not worship the God thou speakest of; neither do I call upon his Name; for I have made to myself a God, which abideth alway in mine House, and provideth me with all Things.

8. And Abraham's Zeal was kindled against the Man; and he arose, and fell upon him, and drove him forth with Blows into the Wilderness.

9. And at Midnight God called unto Abraham, saying, Abraham, where is the Stranger?

10. And Abraham answered and said, Lord, he would not worship thee, neither would he call upon thy Name; therefore have I driven him out from before my Face into the Wilderness.

11. And God said, Have I born with him these hundred ninety and eight Years, and nourished him, and cloathed him, notwithstanding his Rebellion against me, and couldst not thou, that art thyself a Sinner, bear with him one Night?

12. And Abraham said, Let not the Anger of my Lord wax hot against his Servant. Lo, I have sinned; forgive me, I pray Thee.

13. And Abraham arose and went forth into the Wilderness, and sought diligently for the Man, and found him, and returned with him to

his Tent; and when he had entreated him kindly,
he sent him away on the Morrow with Gifts.

14. And God spake again unto Abraham,
saying, For this thy Sin shall thy Seed be
afflicted four Hundred Years in a strange Land:

15. But for thy Repentance will I deliver
them; and they shall come forth with Power,
and with Gladness of Heart, and with much
Substance.

Franklin regretted, he wrote late in life, the fame
the "Parable" acquired through frequent publication
because it deprived him "of a good deal of amuse-
ment, which I used to take in reading it by heart
out of my Bible, and obtaining the remarks of the
Scriptuarians upon it, which were sometimes very
diverting; not but that it is in itself, on account
of the importance of its moral, well worth being
made known to all mankind." In the spirit of
*The Spectator* Franklin sought to spice morality
with wit, making the former less austere and the
latter more useful.

As part of his lifelong campaign for religious
toleration and to encourage churches to foster good
works in men, Franklin sought frequently to add
breadth and humor to the religion of his relatives
in Boston. In response to his sister's admonition
about his alleged atheism, Franklin defended his
own faith and observed that "there are some
Things in your New England Doctrines and Worship, which I do not agree with, but I do not
therefore condemn them, or desire to shake your
Belief or Practice of them. We may dislike things
that are nevertheless right in themselves. I would
only have you make me the same Allowances, and
have a better Opinion both of Morality and your
Brother . . . when you judge of others. if you can
perceive the Fruit to be good, don't terrify your
self that the Tree may be evil, but be assur'd it is

not so; for you know who has said, *Men do not gather Grapes of Thorns or Figs of Thistles.*"

In 1745 Franklin teased his brother John about the vast quantity of prayers (forty-five million in four or five months, he calculated) said on behalf of the New England expedition to capture the French fortress at Louisbourg, and their utility in the assault: "If you do not succeed, I fear I shall have but an indifferent opinion of Presbyterian prayers in such cases, as long as I live. Indeed, in attacking strong towns I should have more dependence on *works*, than on *faith* . . . in a French garrison I suppose there are devils . . . that are not to be cast out by prayers and fasting, unless it be by their own fasting for want of provisions. I believe there is Scripture in what I have wrote, but I cannot adorn the margin with quotations, having a bad memory, and no Concordance at hand."

The New England prayers were answered, but Louisbourg was returned to France in the peace treaty, and after its recapture by Britain in 1758, Franklin cautioned his sister: "I congratulate you on the conquest of Cape Breton, and hope as your people took it by praying, the first time, you will now pray that it may never be given up again, which you then forgot." In the same letter Franklin explained a saying which emphasized faith and hope above charity, and then lectured about the comparative merits of those virtues: "*Faith* is the ground floor, *hope* is up one pair of stairs. My dear beloved Jenny, don't delight so much to dwell in those lower rooms, but get as fast as you can into the garret, for in truth the best room in the house is *charity*. For my part, I wish the house was turned upside down; 'tis so difficult (when one is fat) to go upstairs; and not only so, but I imagine *hope* and *faith* may be more firmly built on *charity*, than *charity* upon *faith* and *hope*."

Upon his brother John's death after a long, pain-

ful illness, Franklin wrote tenderly to a mourning
stepdaughter:

> Why . . . should we grieve that a new child
> is born among the immortals? A new member
> added to their happy society? We are spirits.
> That bodies should be lent us, while they can
> afford us pleasure, assist us in acquiring knowl-
> edge, or doing good to our fellow creatures, is
> a kind and benevolent act of God—when they
> become unfit for these purposes and afford us
> pain instead of pleasure—instead of an aid,
> become an incumbrance and answer none of the
> intentions for which they were given, it is
> equally kind and benevolent that a way is
> provided by which we may get rid of them.
> Death is that way. . . . He that quits the whole
> body, parts at once with all pains and possibili-
> ties of pains and diseases it was liable to, or
> capable of making him suffer.
>    Our friend [John Franklin] and we are in-
> vited abroad on a party of pleasure—that is
> to last for ever. His chair was first ready and
> he is gone before us. We could not all con-
> veniently start together, and why should you
> and I be grieved at this, since we are soon to
> follow, and we know where to find him.

Though Franklin was doubtless concerned more
to console his young relative than to be perfectly
precise about his own beliefs, he was not wholly
hypocritical, and the letter underscores his acceptance, frequently expressed, of the *positive* aspects
of Christianity: attention to good works, consola-
tion to the afflicted, concern for human welfare,
and the like.

In 1790, a month before his death, Franklin wrote
to Ezra Stiles, president of Yale College and his
friend for forty years, summarizing his religious
views and at the same time displaying his easy, al-

most flippant attitude toward some weighty questions:

You desire to know something of my Religion. It is the first time I have been questioned upon it. But I cannot take your Curiosity amiss, and shall endeavour in a few Words to gratify it. Here is my Creed. I believe in one God, Creator of the Universe. That he governs it by his Providence. That he ought to be worshipped. That the most acceptable Service we render to him is doing good to his other Children. That the soul of Man is immortal, and will be treated with Justice in another Life respecting its Conduct in this. These I take to be the fundamental Principles of all sound Religion, and I regard them as you do in whatever Sect I meet with them.

As to Jesus of Nazareth, my Opinion of whom you particularly desire, I think the System of Morals and his Religion, as he left them to us, the best the World ever saw or is likely to see; but I apprehend it has received various corrupting Changes, and I have, with most of the present Dissenters in England, some Doubts as to his Divinity; tho' it is a question I do not dogmatize upon, having never studied it, and think it needless to busy myself with it now, when I expect soon an Opportunity of knowing the Truth with less Trouble. I see no harm, however, in its being believed, if that Belief has the good Consequence, as probably it has, of making his Doctrines more respected and better observed; especially as I do not perceive, that the Supreme takes it amiss, by distinguishing the Unbelievers in his Government of the World with any peculiar Marks of his Displeasure.

I shall only add, respecting myself, that, having experienced the Goodness of that Being

in conducting me prosperously thro' a long life,
I have no doubt of its Continuance in the next,
though without the smallest Conceit of meriting
such Goodness. . . .

I confide, that you will not expose me to
Criticism and censure by publishing any part
of this Communication to you. I have ever let
others enjoy their religious Sentiments, without
reflecting on them for those that appeared to
me unsupportable and even absurd. All Sects
here, and we have a great Variety, have experienced my good will in assisting them with
Subscriptions for building their new Places of
Worship; and, as I have never opposed any of
their Doctrines, I hope to go out of the World
in Peace with them all.

The near identity of this creed, expressed in
Franklin's eighty-fifth year with that formulated
when he was twenty-two leaves little doubt that his
settled religious belief was a conventional deism.
Thousands, perhaps millions, of men alert to the
new thought of the eighteenth century would have
accepted the articles he proposed for the "United
Party of Virtue" and restated for Ezra Stiles sixty
years later. Franklin was neither unique nor creative
as a religious thinker. His brief, unsatisfactory
attempt at polemical writing, the sophomoric essay
on liberty and necessity printed in 1725, seems to
have convinced him that such endeavor was point-
less. In proving that "whatever is is right" and that
man could not be held responsible for his actions,
Franklin merely showed himself, since he did not
believe his syllogistic conclusions, that fine-spun
arguments do not always lead to wisdom. He knew
that there were some things that "were" that were
not right (that, after all, is why he sponsored civic
*improvements* in Philadelphia), and he held men,
including himself, accountable for their conduct.

Franklin's deism, eclectic, not always consistent,

and sometimes neglectful of dilemmas, allowed him
to make an easy reconciliation between the new
skeptical thought he adhered to intellectually and
the generous humanitarianism his childhood training and adult experience insisted upon. It was a
faith to live by rather than to speculate on or
agonize over. Since he did not bother to re-examine
it fundamentally after his early manhood, he left
no profound works questing or probing for religious
insight. As he said repeatedly, he would not waste
his energy splitting theological hairs.

   In refusing to debate religious questions, in his
pragmatic attitude, and in his occasional flippancy,
Franklin left himself exposed to charges of hypocrisy. Was he not saying, critics asked, in pro-
claiming all doctrinal disputes foolish, that it didn't
make any difference whether, for example, the
Bible was the word of God or Jesus divine? Wasn't
his hypocrisy compounded when, after ridiculing
the polemicists, he nevertheless asserted the utility
of religion, supported churches, and encouraged his
friends and relatives to believe in doctrines he made
sport of with his skeptical friends? To many earnest
and conscientious people Franklin seemed to be
encouraging people to believe in what was not
true, and to be willing to countenance error for
the sake of its social utility in controlling those
more stupid or less secure than himself. At times
Franklin seemed close to endorsing the Marxist
notion that "religion is the opiate of the people";
that it would "chain the tyger" in men, making
them docile laborers in the oppressive system of the
cynical masters of thought control.
   Franklin was sincere in his own beliefs, however,
and he had no devious or ulterior motives in wanting
others to remain secure in their various faiths.
Though his own statements about religion were
often conventional and even perfunctory, there is
no evidence that he made them cynically. In fact,

by staying away from church when he thought the
preacher would say nothing useful or edifying,
Franklin was a good deal more candid than many
bored or unbelieving churchgoers. There is no reason to suppose, just because his conclusions about
religion were conventional (though unorthodox),
that his consistent, lifelong deism was a cowardly
mask to cover his lack of conviction. Franklin persisted in his faith and over and over again wrote
unaffectedly and persuasively about it.

His belief in the social value of the religions he
knew about in America was similarly sincere.
Though he wrote eloquently in favor of toleration
and fought every kind of religious persecution, it is
significant that of established churches he asked
only that they permit freedom of worship to dissenters. He believed, as did those who supported
Establishments, that religion was an essential prop
to public morality, and he favored institutions which
strengthened that morality. Franklin was scarcely
less convinced than Aquinas or Calvin that strong
religious faith was the essential foundation of a
good society. He differed from them and other
zealots principally in believing that a variety of
religions, all teaching acceptable morality, could
serve as well as or better than one religion in under-
girding the public welfare. He had little use for the
complicated theories of church and state which had
troubled philosophers for centuries, but he had a
strong sense of the good churches did in the communities where he lived. The thrifty, prudential,
neighborly communities he always admired in New
England had their foundations, he knew, in the
Puritan faith, and the benevolence of Quakers in
Philadelphia, which contributed so much to the
welfare of that city, confirmed Franklin's opinion
of the positive connection between religion and
the good society. When men of faith shunned mere
cant and polemics and instead taught virtue and

morality, they could depend on Franklin's whole-hearted support.

A charge more serious than that impugning the sincerity of Franklin's religion and his attitude toward it has to do with his bland shallowness in treating weighty and intricate religious matters. He proposed a revision of the Lord's Prayer, for example, substituting "Heavenly father, May all revere thee, and become thy dutiful Children and faithful Subjects," for "Our Father which art in Heaven, Hallowed be thy Name. Thy Kingdom come." Besides the presumption of the effort, one wonders if the new version is any better, a doubt not put to rest by Franklin's "Reasons for the Change of Expression." "Heavenly Father" was preferred because it "is more concise, equally expressive, and better modern English," and "hallowed be thy Name" is discarded because modern Englishmen did not have any proper "Name" for God as the ancient Jews did, and besides, "the Word *hallowed* is almost obsolete." Finally, the word "Kingdom" had to go because it referred to an ancient theocracy which no longer existed. Franklin also revised, shortened, and modernized the Psalms and the Book of Common Prayer. Though these efforts reflect something of the spirit of later revisers of the language of the Bible, Franklin's smugness exposes his irreverence for the subject matter. To him it was more important to be concise, modern, and pedantic than to preserve hallowed forms and respect a cadence and imagery which were an important part of the worship performed in the prayer.

Just as the poetry of Addison and Pope lacks the spiritual grandeur of Milton or Donne, and does not match the mystical insight of Wordsworth or Coleridge, Franklin failed to express anything like the religious profundity which characterized the ages which preceded and followed his own. By his day the earnestness and vigor of the Puritans in tackling fundamental questions of man's existence, and the brilliance of the writing which resulted, had hardened into the sterile polemics which disgusted Franklin. Issues which were intense and lively when argued by John Bunyan in Bedford, near the Franklin ancestral home in England, seemed stale and irrelevant when re-argued by Benjamin Franklin's Presbyterian minister in Philadelphia. Franklin turned his intensity outward to matters of civic improvement and he transformed the Puritan's incessant introspection of the soul into a clever game of moral self-examination recorded on handy tablets. That he thought of his exercise as a substitute for the Puritan introspection, and even an improvement on it, is highly probable; that it yielded as profound a moral awareness or as deep a spiritual insight is less certain.

There were realms of experience and meaning that Franklin and most other Enlightenment thinkers simply did not probe. What becomes of Franklin's sweet reasonableness in facing the problems of man and society when set beside Augustine's *City of God*—or even Reinhold Niebuhr's *Moral Man and Immoral Society?* What becomes of Franklin's world view when held up against the insights of Freud and William Faulkner? It is unfair to brand Franklin with all the superficialities and overconfidences of what Carl Becker has aptly called "The Heavenly City of the Eighteenth Century Philosophers"—he drank of life too deeply to be tricked by the musings of closet philosophers—but in his fidelity to his age he nevertheless missed some of the paradoxes and complexities of the human condition.

For example, in the letter quoted above recommending suppression of the atheistical tract, Franklin recognized that for many men, perhaps for most, a conscious self-discipline and an adult reason would not furnish the habits and values necessary for a virtuous life. He even noted that the writer, who prided himself on his own standards of good conduct, did not *acquire* the habits necessary to uphold those standards through application of his system of natural ethics. Those habits came, Franklin guessed, from his "Religious Education." Now, exactly that line of reasoning applies to Franklin himself, something he knew very well but seems never to have considered sufficiently in his general reflections on society. His own "Tyger" had been "chained" by his wise, firm, and pious father when day after day the older man formed his son's habits, reactions, and outlook on life with a mixture of advice, admonition, encouragement, scolding, instruction, and discipline which, in spite of a full share of youthful indiscretions, left Franklin inclined to deal with life honestly and earnestly. If this was true in his own case, it is surprising he proposed to "chain the Tyger" in other men with such a superficial scheme as his art of virtue.

To put it another way, Franklin lived all his life on the dividends from the large stock of moral capital his father had drawn from his religious faith. Though Benjamin Franklin retained a large measure of the profits (virtue), he cut himself off from his father's supplying bank. Was it wise to suppose the flow of dividends would continue for generations to come? Furthermore, he seemed at times to assume that men in general, most of whom may have had little or no connection with the kind of discipline which reigned in the Franklin household in Boston, had passions and impulses no more ungovernable than his own subdued and directed ones. The porous sands of overconfidence in human nature and oversimplification of social problems which critics have seen under Franklin's thought may have been deposited there by his failure to see the full implications of his own close connection with the great value-conserving institutions of his native land.

Franklin's inability or at best unwillingness to

partake of deep spiritual experience suggests that he was not antireligious, as his critics have charged, but merely in a sense nonreligious. His conventional deism, his unwillingness to reopen fundamental religious questions, his indifference to theology and even to poetry, and his inclination to treat matters of faith and dogma with playful humor all bespeak a certain limitation in his range of interest. This is not to say that Franklin was prosaic, or lacked imagination or passion or intensity of feeling. He simply directed those energies to tangible concerns; his *zeal* to understand lightning showed great *imagination* and his *passion* for civic improvement left a profound mark on Philadelphia. It is nevertheless true, however, that vast and wondrous realms of human experience and endeavor were untouched by Franklin, and would remain febrile and impoverished if all genius was channeled as his was.

# Chapter XI

# The Public Philosophy
# of a Sage

WHEN FRANKLIN CAME home in 1785, there was a clear call for his talent and wisdom in seeking "the unearned increment created by human accord": the newly independent United States needed desperately "to form a more perfect union." Franklin did not bring profound political theory or even any particular talent for devising institutions of government to this exacting task. He brought what was most needed in the aftermath of revolution where the premium had been on ringing words, reckless courage, and persistence in principle: the wisdom of experience, the good sense of a sage, and an unfailing instinct for proposing the next short step men might take in agreement, or at least in agreement to disagree.

During the Constitutional Convention, which met in Philadelphia in the summer of 1787, a respite from gout and bladder-stone attacks permitted Franklin to serve as a member of the Pennsylvania delegation. He told his sister that he "attended the Business of [the Convention] 5 Hours in every Day from the beginning, which is something more than four Months . . . my Health continues; some tell me I look better, and they suppose the daily Exercise of going and returning from the Statehouse has done me good." Twenty years older than any of the delegates, most of whom were under forty, he was characterized by William Pierce:

> Dr. Franklin is well known to be the greatest philosopher of the present age;—all the operations of nature he seems to understand, the very heavens obey him, and the clouds yield up their Lightning to be imprisoned in his rod . . . It is certain that he does not shine much in public Council, he is no Speaker, nor does he seem to let politics engage his attention. He is, however, a most extraordinary Man, and tells a story in a style more engaging than anything I ever heard. . . . He is 82 years old, and possesses an activity of mind equal to a youth of 25.

Franklin came to the Convention convinced that stronger articles of union were needed and armed with suggestions for a well-ordered government, but his chief contribution was not as a proposer of ideas or as a director of debate. He served most importantly as conciliator. Every delegate knew of his vast experience in public affairs and expected him, at critical moments, to interject sage advice or to sound a soothing note of good humor. His presence reminded members that in spite of her newness as a nation, America possessed at least one citizen whose wisdom was acknowledged as unsurpassed anywhere in the world. He gave them the courage to have great expectations.

Franklin's contributions in the debates were always to particular points, often brief admonitions resting on some particular experience, and usually were illustrated with an example or anecdote. When the Convention rejected his proposals (which it did frequently), his colleagues showed great respect for their author and usually found a way to lay them aside without direct challenge. Franklin urged, for example, that the executive officers receive no

salary because "there are two passions which have
a powerful influence on the affairs of men . . . the
love of power, and the love of money . . . When
united in view of the same object, they have in
many minds the most violent effects. . . . The
struggles for [offices of profit] are the true sources
of all those factions which are perpetually dividing
[Great Britain], distracting its councils, hurrying it
sometimes into fruitless and mischievous wars, and
often compelling a submission to dishonourable
terms of peace." Paying officers, Franklin continued,
would tend to fill places with greedy men who, once
entrenched, might intrigue for a monarchy in order
to stay in office. He then gave examples of corruption caused by profit-seekers in government, and
cited cases where good and honorable men had served
in public stations without pay, observing that "the
pleasure of doing good and serving their Country
and the respect such conduct entitles them to, are
sufficient motives with some minds to give up a
great portion of their time to the Public, without
the mean inducement of pecuniary satisfaction."
Alexander Hamilton seconded the proposal to bring
it before the Convention, but no debate ensued and
the motion was postponed. James Madison recorded
that "it was treated with great respect, but rather
for the author of it, than from any apparent conviction of its expediency or practicality." Two days
later. Franklin opposed giving the executive an
absolute veto, citing abuses of that power by the
proprietary governors of Pennsylvania and the stad-
holders in the Netherlands, and at another time he
sought to prohibit re-election of the president as a
guard against tyranny. He seldom argued in support
of his suggestions, being content generally to let the
Convention dispose of them as it saw fit.

Over and over again, though, fervently and on
the whole effectively, he pleaded for a spirit of com-

promise and a willingness to listen and learn. He opened his speech opposing salaries with the remark that "the Committee will judge of my reasons when they have heard them, and their judgment may possibly change mine." When it appeared that debate over representation would become acrimonious, Franklin called for calm tempers:

> We are sent here to *consult*, not to *contend*, with each other; and declarations of a fixed opinion, and of determined resolution, never to change it, neither enlighten nor convince us. Positiveness and warmth on one side, naturally beget their like on the other; and tend to create and augment discord and division in a great concern, wherein harmony and Union are extremely necessary to give weight to our Councils, and render them effectual in promoting and securing the common good.

Late in June, during very hot weather, when Washington "despaired of seeing a favorable issue to the proceedings," Franklin made his famous proposal that the Convention open its sessions with prayer. He observed that without God's aid

> . . . we shall succeed in this political building no better than the Builders of Babel: We shall be divided by our little partial local interests; our projects will be confounded, and we ourselves shall become a reproach and bye word down to future ages. And what is worse, mankind may hereafter from this unfortunate instance, despair of establishing Governments by Human Wisdom and leave it to chance, war and conquest.

Though the proposal was not adopted, tempers seemed to cool and a few days later, upon Franklin's motion, the "great compromise" was agreed upon: the states to be represented equally in the Senate and the people to be equal in the House.

To fulfill his role as conciliator, Franklin told stories in and out of doors. One time, when two opposing members had insisted on receiving all they contended for, he asked them to remember that "When a broad table is to be made, and the edges of the plank do not fit the artist takes a little from both, and makes a good joint." At another time, when a group of delegates had gathered for tea under a mulberry tree in the courtyard of his new house near Independence Hall, he showed them a phial containing a two-headed snake. He cautioned that the reptile, if its heads took opposite sides of a stalk on the way to a stream, might die of thirst unless the difference were accommodated. Franklin understood that knowledge of history, learning in the law, and brilliant political theories were not enough to resolve great questions of statecraft, and that there will always be differences of opinion among free men gathered in deliberative assembly. Compromise, then, was essential and required the kind of courage Poor Richard had spoken of long ago: "The wise and the brave dares own he was wrong."

In four months' debate, the Convention hammered out a draft constitution. On the day set for its final approval, Franklin addressed to the members a plea that, despite misgivings, they all sign the document. That speech, Franklin's last in public, put in unforgettable words his final counsel of wisdom for his country and was soon reprinted in newspapers throughout the nation, having an effect on the ratification debates far exceeding that of *The Federalist* papers and probably greater than that of any contribution to the discussions. It is quoted here in full to display Franklin's habits of mind at their best:

I confess that I do not entirely approve of this Constitution at present, but Sir, I am not sure I shall never approve it: For having lived long, I have experienced many Instances of being oblig'd, by better Information or fuller Consideration, to change Opinions even on important Subjects, which I once thought right, but found to be otherwise. It is therefore that the older I grow the more apt I am to doubt my own Judgment, and to pay more Respect to the Judgment of others. Most Men indeed as well as most Sects in Religion, think themselves in Possession of all Truth, and that wherever others differ from them it is so far Error. Steele, a Protestant in a Dedication tells the Pope, that the only Difference between our two Churches in their Opinions of the Certainty of their Doctrine, is, the Romish Church is infallible, and the Church of England is never in the Wrong. But tho' many private Persons think almost as highly of their own Infallibility, as of that of their Sect, few express it so naturally as a certain French Lady, who in a little Dispute with her Sister, said, I don't know how it happens, Sister, but I meet with no body but myself that's *always* in the right. *Il n'y a que moi qui a toujours raison.*

In these Sentiments, Sir, I agree to this Constitution, with all its Faults, if they are such; because I think a General Government necessary for us, and there is no *Form* of Government but what may be a Blessing to the People if well administred; and I believe farther that this is likely to be well administred for a Course of Years, and can only end in Despotism as other Forms have done before it, when the People shall become so corrupted as to need Despotic Government, being incapable of any other. I doubt too whether any other Convention we can obtain, may be able to make a better

Constitution: For when you assemble a Number of Men to have the Advantage of their joint Wisdom, you inevitably assemble with those Men all their Prejudices, their Passions, their Errors of Opinion, their local Interests, and their selfish Views. From such an Assembly can a perfect Production be expected? It therefore astonishes me, Sir, to find this System approaching so near to Perfection as it does; and I think it will astonish our Enemies, who are waiting with Confidence to hear that our Councils are confounded, like those of the Builders of Babel, and that our States are on the Point of Separation, only to meet hereafter for the Purpose of cutting one anothers Throats. Thus I consent, Sir, to this Constitution because I expect no better, and because I am not sure that it is not the best. The opinions I have had of its Errors, I sacrifice to the Public Good. I have never whisper'd a Syllable of them abroad. Within these Walls they were born, and here they shall die. If every one of us in returning to our Constituents were to report the Objections he has had to it, and use his Influence to gain Partizans in support of them, we might prevent its being generally received, and thereby lose all the Salutary Effects and great Advantages resulting naturally in our favour among foreign Nations, as well as among ourselves, from our real or apparent Unanimity. Much of the Strength and Efficiency of any Government, in procuring and securing Happiness to the People depends on Opinion, on the general Opinion of the Goodness of that Government as well as of the Wisdom and Integrity of its Governors. I hope therefore that for our own Sakes as a Part of the People, and for the sake of our Posterity, we shall act heartily and unanimously in recommending this Constitution, wherever our Influence may extend, and turn our future Thoughts and Endeavours to Means of having it well administred.

On the whole, Sir, I cannot help expressing a Wish, that every member of the Convention, who may still have Objections to it, would with me on this Occasion doubt a little of his own Infallibility, and to make *manifest* our *Unanimity*, put his Name to this Instrument.

In this speech Franklin brought the wisdom of a lifetime to bear on the great question, posed by Hamilton in the first *Federalist* paper, facing the country and the world in 1787: "whether societies of men are really capable or not, of establishing good government from reflection and choice, or whether they are forever destined to depend, for their political constitutions, on accident and force." Franklin knew there was no sure answer, either yes or no. He had hoped, at Albany in 1754, that the American colonies and the mother country could agree on a union beneficial to all. To the end of his life he continued to believe that a little more wisdom, a little more forbearance at that time might have preserved the British Empire in peace and freedom. He worked hard to find the accommodations to prevent the Revolutionary War and felt often between 1765 and 1775 that moderation on all sides might have done it. As a scientist he knew that hypotheses had to be tentative pending discovery of new facts; so in public affairs men had to be ready to change their opinions in the light of new evidence or arguments. He knew, too, that men and the societies in which they lived were imperfect; to wait for perfection in human affairs was to wait forever and to lose chance after chance to take the next possible step along the way toward a little bit better today or tomorrow. In urging acceptance of the new Constitution, Franklin advised the only attitude which will permit free men to live together in peace and prosperity: admit of fallibility, be willing to forgo perfection, and take short steps forward when possible.

Though Franklin's main contribution at the Constitutional Convention was to prevent its disruption in failure, he worked at the same time for his own ideas of good government. Among the proposals he put forth or supported were a unicameral legislature, a plural executive, nonpayment of officials, a limited executive veto, provision for impeachment of officeholders, absence of federal property qualifications for voters, representation according to population, liberal naturalization laws, denial of a Senate voice in money bills, ineligibility of the President for re-election, and explicit power to permit federal canal-building. Some of these measures merely reflect pet notions developed in sixty years of close attention to public affairs. Franklin sought a plural executive, for example, to prevent abuses he had observed in arbitrary governors in America and ministers in England, and he wanted to deny the Senate a voice in money bills to avoid the obstruction he had experienced as a member of the Pennsylvania Assembly. By limiting the President to one term, Franklin hoped by rotating officeholders to prevent the rise of a parasitic bureaucracy such as he had come to abhor in England. He supported his suggestions with lessons from history or from his own experience. Machinery for impeaching officials would make the more drastic measure (decapitation) used by Parliament against Charles I unnecessary. He thought liberal naturalization laws good because "we found in the Course of the Revolution that many strangers served us faithfully . . . When foreigners after looking about for some other Country in which they can obtain more happiness, give a preference to ours, it is proof of attachment which ought to excite our confidence and affection."

More significant than these bits of humane sagacity, though, are the repeated revelations of Franklin's belief in government by consent and the capacity of the people to be effective rulers. In favoring lower-house control of money bills he recalled the maxim "that those who feel, can best judge," and that therefore it was wise for "money affairs to be confined to the immediate representatives of the people." To those who thought it humiliating to make the executive ineligible for re-election, he responded that "In free governments the rulers are the servants, and the people their superiors and sovereigns. For the former therefore to return among the latter was not to *degrade* but to *promote* them." He opposed limiting the suffrage to freeholders and setting property qualifications for officeholders because "it is of great consequence that we should not depress the virtue and public spirit of our common people . . . the elected [did not have] any right in any case to narrow the privileges of the electors . . . if honesty were often the companion of wealth, and if poverty was exposed to peculiar temptation, it was not less true that the possession of property increased the desire for more property. Some of the greatest rogues . . . were the richest rogues."

Though the ideal, Franklin thought, was for every member "to consider himself rather as a Representative of the whole, than as an Agent for the interests of a particular State," this outcome was unlikely to be the case, so he proposed as the only fair rule that "the number of Representatives should bear some proportion to the number of Represented; and that decisions should be by the majority of members, not by the majority of States." He believed in 1787, just as he had in 1755 in opposing proprietary rule in Pennsylvania and in 1776 in opposing arbitrary British government in America, that the indispensable conditions of good government were explicit mechanisms for making it responsive to the will and sometimes even to the whims of the people.

Some students of Franklin's thought, quoting these statements and particularly in noticing his support of a unicameral legislature, have seen him as a full-fledged democrat in the modern meaning of that term. A unicameral legislature, elected by the people and unrestrained by an upper house, executive veto, or judicial review, is in the minds of advocates of pure majority rule the only just depository of political power. Though Franklin shared some of this feeling, his experience in the one-house legislature of colonial Pennsylvania was the main source of his support for such a body. It had worked efficiently, was less expensive than maintaining two houses, and furnished less opportunity for devious intrigue. Franklin's mind, always seeking practical simplicity, reacted against the intricate contrivances for checks and balances in government which so fascinated John Adams, for example. In Philadelphia Franklin had been used to dealing with community affairs as directly and efficiently as possible; it was only common sense, he felt, to conduct a general government similarly.

But Franklin was no simple majoritarian democrat believing that the only meaningful standard for any public measure was its conformity to majority will. He believed that the people, properly educated and inculcated with a concern for the public welfare, would on the whole exercise their franchise wisely, or at least come to measures less objectionable than those likely to result from any other existing government or any which could be projected. But he had no more faith in mobs, "the masses," or the virtue of rude men than the rest of the delegates to the Constitutional Convention. To him "democracy" was an epithet. It meant, as it had for educated men at least since Aristotle's day, the rule by the masses, or the "lower orders," swayed by demagogues and guided by the most violent and capricious passions.

Franklin had clearly in his mind Thucydides' picture of the conduct of the enraged "commons" during the Corcyraean revolution: they "engaged in butchering those of their fellow citizens whom they regarded as their enemies: and although the crime imputed was that of attempting to put down the democracy, some were slain also for private hatred, others by their debtors because of monies owed them. Death thus raged in every shape; and as usually happens at such times, there was no length to which violence did not go; sons were kill'd by their fathers, and suppliants dragged from the altar or slain upon it; while some were even walled up in the temple of Dionysus and died there." To the Enlightenment Man of Reason, devoted to the calm pursuit of the common weal through study and deliberation, such visions, almost always associated with democracy in the eighteenth century, were abhorrent. Franklin, like Jefferson and Madison, believed that only the virtues of the forum could sustain good government.

While he disdained majoritarian democracy, Franklin's concept of the state was not merely negative. He did not agree with men of little faith who could see no powers safely exercised by government, or with those who thought the public welfare consisted in giving private interest and private property unlimited freedom. Raised in community-conscious Boston and an active citizen of the City of Brotherly Love, Franklin was convinced that man's obligation to the society in which he lived had the highest call on his energy and resources. In the last year of his life, Franklin wrote:

The accumulation of Property in Society, and its Security to Individuals must be an Effect of the Protection afforded to it by the joint Strength of the Society, in the Execution of its Laws. Private Property therefore is a Creature of Society, and is subject to the Calls of that Society, whenever its Necessities shall require it, even to its last Farthing; its Contributions therefore to the publick Exigencies are not to be considered as conferring a Benefit on the Publick, entitling the Contributors to the Distinctions of Honour and Power, but as the Return of an Obligation previously received, or the Payment of a just Debt. The Combinations of Civil Society are not like those of a Set of Merchants, who club their property in different Proportions for Building and Freighting a Ship, and may therefore have some Right to vote in the Disposition of the Voyage in a greater or lesser Degree according to their respective Contributions; but the important ends of Civil Society, and the personal Securities of Life and Liberty, those remain the same in every Member of the society; and the poorest continues to have an equal Claim to them with the most opulent, whatever Difference Time, Chance, or Industry may occasion in their Circumstances.

At the heart of Franklin's public philosophy, then, was neither a belief in majority rule plain and simple nor a fear of any and all power in government, but rather a conviction that there were good and better standards, which, in seeking, men might in whatever measure they chose, exercise civil power. Even more than many men of his day with college educations, all of whom had been exposed, directly or indirectly, to Aristotle's *Politics*, Franklin took to heart the Greek's maxims that "man is a political animal" and that though the state may come into existence for "the bare needs of life, [it] continued in existence for the sake of the good life." No aspect of modern political understanding separates us more from the mode of thought of Franklin and the other founding fathers than our tacit assumption of relative values and their tacit assumption that on earth as in the heavens, in the affairs of men as in nature, there were eternal verities, which in politics were called natural rights.

It is characteristic of twentieth-century political thought that so much energy has been expended to refute the doctrine of natural rights. They are, we are told, merely specific privileges bestowed by certain societies on certain of their members. In any case, no rights can be natural (universally applicable to all men) since, as the anthropologists have shown, there are no customs, habits, or beliefs which are common to all cultures. Historians and social scientists have written countless volumes to show that what men of Franklin's day asserted were natural rights, especially those related to property, were nothing more than clever codes to make the rich richer and the poor poorer, and that natural law was a notion devised to inflict the mores of a ruling class of a particular society on the rest of the world. Under heavy pressure, modern thought has retreated from one certainty after another until "everything is relative" has become a cliché in our climate of opinion, serious scholars debate whether even "relativity" can be "absolute," and college sophomores, applauded by their teachers, commonly go through a phase of doubting everything and finding old assurances hopelessly outmoded and themselves adrift in "a meaningless void."

To all of this Franklin would in a way have been sympathetic. He was an intrepid doubter and suffered many calumnies on that account. In response to his speech urging acceptance of the Constitution, an antifederalist writer in a Boston newspaper remarked acidly that "the doubting *Doctor*, who has been remarkable for skepticism from fourteen to four score," should doubt the new Constitution. Franklin sought diligently for new truths, kept hypotheses tentative as an article of faith, and urged in science and elsewhere, when disputes arose, "let the experiment be made." He was in many respects the most "modern" man of his generation, deserving the title "the first American pragmatist" bestowed repeatedly upon him. It is hard to imagine any contemporary scientist, social or otherwise, or any follower of John Dewey, objecting to Franklin's habitual approach to particular problems. He gathered evidence, made observations, formulated hypotheses, tested them, rejected them when proved wrong, and settled on others, expecting that in due time they, too, would fall before new evidence. But as a believer in the Newtonian world view, Franklin had a radically different concept of the persistent direction and ultimate nature of physical and social forces than that common today. He assumed, as did many intellectuals of his day, that morality and social understanding, though lagging behind natural science, would follow it through progressive stages of enlightenment and rationalization, and would end finally a part of a marvelously harmonious whole. Franklin did not believe social theorists could point the way to the perfect society as did some of his contemporaries, but in a serene, patient way, he viewed himself and his activities on behalf of human welfare as part of a grand, irresistible movement toward a better world.

Franklin was confident of this progress because he was sure his age had discovered the eternal verities —natural rights—of enlightened politics. Though he and his contemporaries took the natural rights too much for granted to have spent much time trying to define them, they would have agreed that they included the rights to personal freedom, to some form of franchise, to freedom of belief and discussion, to revolt against tyrannical governments, and to national independence. The eighteenth-century climate of opinion would have nodded to quibbles over definition and to the arguments about the restrictions nearly always surrounding these rights, but it would not have thought that the limitations in any significant way abridged the importance or universality of the rights. Franklin lived in an age which for the most part had not yet accepted David Hume's insight that the empirical method popularized by Locke could prove little about cause and effect. The separation thus introduced between the atomized world of sense experience and the systematic realm of ideas and natural law had little place in Franklin's world view.

Following Hume, it is now common to point out the contradiction between the seventeenth- and eighteenth-century fascination with the observable facts of nature in all their infinite variety, and the laws which Newton proposed showing how all phenomena had systematic cause-and-effect relationships. Using the empirical method, according to Hume, when one observed one billiard ball hit another, one could say nothing about the first having *caused* the second to move; one could say merely that the first moved in such-and-such way, and that the second moved in such-and-such different fashion. By implication, religion, morality, politics, and other more weighty matters were subject to similarly random analysis. This subtle understanding, and its corrosive effect on both man's sense that the universe was intelligible and harmonious and his inclination to see government as responsible to immutable concepts of justice and reason, had little impact on Franklin. He and most of his colleagues in American nation-building accepted easily what twentieth-century understanding often finds inconsistent: that one could have a thoroughly empirical approach to the natural world and at the same time have confidence in the harmony of the universe and its progress, according to rational laws, toward moral and social improvement if not perfection.

This serene hopefulness, added to the freedom-loving, open-ended attitude nourished by life in the new world and a willingness to use civil power to seek the good life, form the essential components of Franklin's public philosophy. The unfolding pattern of his life suggests both how he came to this philosophy and how it might be relevant today. As a youth he had been trained carefully in the personal virtues: honesty, industry, thrift, humility, temperance, charity, and the rest. He learned to respect the values which had allowed Christian to complete successfully the pilgrimage to the Celestial City. He was, in short, a good person before he was anything else. Then, arriving in Philadelphia full of zest to make his way in the world, he plunged into making a living for himself and his family and at the same time entwined his personal welfare with that of his fellow citizens. He began immediately, especially through the Junto, to exert what influence he could to improve his city. The Library, the Fire Company, the Academy, and the Hospital were all founded on that impulse. He learned how to take personal virtues and mold them, through voluntary association, into institutions of community betterment. It was perfectly natural to him to apply the personal obligations he had learned as a youth to the wider civic sphere. He never doubted that the good qualities of individuals, writ large, became the means of social progress. This experience and insight gave him the essential foundation for his emergence into the more critical political arena. As a civic promoter he had had no legal power over those not inclined to follow his lead. In seeking or accepting public office he crossed the fateful line from being a mere projector to being able at times to *perpetrate* his programs on others through the unique compulsive authority of the state.

In crossing the line, though, he did not conceive that he needed to change either his intentions or his habits. He still had in mind seeking the common welfare and he still supposed it essential to exercise the goodwill and dexterity in human relations he had learned in thirty years as a tradesman and civic leader. His public philosophy, then, was a projection of the personal virtues he had been trained to as a boy and had learned to extend to the cooperative enterprises of Philadelphia citizenship. In opposing arbitrary British rule in America, Franklin merely applied to the colonies at large the cardinal tenet of his own life: all people have a right to direct their own destinies. His faith in the benefits of union applied to the colonies collectively advantages he had observed in forming associations for civic improvement. In seeking, honestly and sincerely, French aid for the rebelling colonies, Franklin simply projected to international relations habits and attitudes he had learned were effective in forty years of negotiations of all kinds. In fostering a spirit of compromise at the Constitutional Convention, he applied maxims of human relations and public affairs his father had found essential in church business in Boston and he himself had used countless times in Philadelphia, London, and Paris. In short, his understanding of men and society, acquired largely through experience, constituted his public philosophy.

Franklin's public philosophy, then, which he never set down systematically, began with the assumption, shared by most of his colleagues in revolution and nation-building, that the values of a good individual life had political relevance: through the right ideas and right conduct of both governed and governors, the public life would be given the indispensable quality of virtue. Franklin would not have entertained the notion that personal values were socially irrelevant or that there were no standards of good conduct to which public affairs might be expected to measure up. In fact, the qualities Christian displayed in *Pilgrim's Progress*, the earnestness Daniel Defoe urged in *Essay on Projects*, and the humane goodwill of *The Spectator* were more than merely relevant to politics; they were vital to the good society. Examples of great and noble conduct on the stage of history, described by Plutarch and others, were worthy of emulation. No question would have been more out of place in the Pennsylvania State House (Independence Hall) in 1755 or 1776 or 1787 than the one so often voiced by the narrowly specialized or relativist habits of modern thought: Is there any substantial concept of the good life which we can use as a guide in public affairs? Franklin would have answered unhesitatingly, "Yes," and he and his colleagues would, whatever their quarrels, have found large areas of agreement as to its flesh and bones. The substance would have been remarkably close to the guiding principles of the Junto Franklin had formed in Philadelphia in 1727.

A belief that there were standards of both means and ends to which a society could aspire meant it was natural to think of the citizen and the governor (ultimately, of course, in democratic societies the offices are combined) as having political obligations; that is, they shared a responsibility to define and to seek those standards. The key word is "obligation" —a duty, a commitment, a moral imperative, to have methods and goals consistent with the values and way of life of the members of the community in mind in the conduct of their government. Franklin would not have supposed for a moment that the personal values of those in government were of no significance in fulfilling their official obligations. They were, in fact, the essential guideposts for settling upon public policy. Franklin understood that fulfillment of his political obligation as a citizen required him to *ask the proper questions;* that is, to have a point of reference outside his own personal desires, to ask not what he or even his city or state could *get* from government, but rather to ask moral questions: what *should* the ends and values of a society be, and what steps *should* the society take to seek them?*

---

* Joseph Tussman, *Obligation and the Body Politic* (New York, 1960), offers a full explanation of this concept in a modern context.

The only way, of course, Franklin could deal intelligently with public questions requiring such judgments was to have in his *own mind and heart* values which he could project upon them. It followed that there had to be a large stock of such values in a large portion of any community which aspired to both democratic government and good government. An acceptance of this need to project personal virtue and values into public life in order to make government more than merely democratic or more, even, than merely free was axiomatic to Franklin as it was to the other great founders, Washington, Jefferson, Adams, Hamilton, and Madison.

If we remember this point of view of Franklin's, some aspects of his understanding of the goals or purpose of the United States of America become apparent. The national purpose was to give form and reality to values shared widely by members of the body politic. These common values included the precepts of Poor Richard, the habits which had enabled Franklin and his neighbors to carry out one civic improvement after another in Philadelphia, and the fundamentals of government declared in 1776 and embodied in a constitution eleven years later. However hard it may have been, and still is, to define more precisely the purpose of the nation, its foes as well as its friends seemed to recognize that there *was* a substance to it. George III did not like it and consequently led a fight against it, whereas Lafayette learned quickly to admire it and spent a lifetime in its cause.

Franklin saw no reason to be dogmatic about the role government should or should not play in seeking the national purpose. Its function was to pursue the ends inherent in the common values of the community in ways which not only did not debauch them but instead enhanced and brightened them in the process. Ideally this suggests a self-guided answer to perennial questions of American politics: What should the powers of government be? Should they

be thought of negatively or positively? Should the
Constitution be interpreted broadly or narrowly?
What of states' rights? Franklin thought of good
government as possessing both self-restraint and a
capacity to implement; to have debated whether the
negative or positive function was primary would not
have occurred to him. He would have been puzzled
by the dispute between backers of the New Deal and
the Liberty League during the 1930's; to have worried about an abstract, doctrinaire definition of the
powers of government would to him have seemed
a poor use of energy. To be effective in seeking a
good society, government had both to be an efficient, authoritative agency for *doing things* and
to show restraint in extending its powers in ways
which interfered with the national purpose. The
government, then, did not *embody* the national purpose, as has often been asserted in totalitarian
states, but rather, properly conceived, it stood ready
to do whatever the community wanted it to do. To
one with Franklin's confidence in the rewards of
social accord, of course, there were a multitude of
important, continuing projects to which government
could and should give powerful support.

A government thus conceived, Franklin felt, had
the essentials of its foreign policy marked out. As the
citizens sought, continuously, to define and realize
standards and goals for themselves, using their government as an instrument, the implications of the
quest would project readily beyond the national
boundaries, but would be unlikely to be hostile or
aggressive. Dangerous international adventures arise
most persistently in nations that have turned pent-
up and frustrated energies outward in the face of
unsolved internal problems. Franklin's letters while
minister to France show his confidence that a nation with the constructive values he thought guided
the new United States was unlikely to be either
neurotically isolationist or compulsively aggressive.
The concern should be to understand how its own

purpose related to other people's and then to seek
relationships consistent with that end.

Franklin's self-consciousness about the purpose of
the United States made him zealous for it to exert
an influence in the world, but at the same time he
saw no need to be a bully, the natural posture of the
fearful and the uncertain. A country intent on its
own search for freedom, to mention one national
purpose, and aware of its position in the vanguard
of that quest in the world, would, Franklin was sure,
have a broad impact in international affairs. This
desire to play a positive role lay behind the warnings
he gave, later echoed by Washington and Jefferson,
to avoid alliances and commitments which would
draw the nation into "the vortex" of Europe's irrelevant squabbles. He believed, as George Kennan has
put it in the middle of the twentieth century, that
the purposes of the United States "are on balance
worthy ones, which can be pursued and achieved
without injury to any other people," and that "the
conduct of its foreign relations [ought not to
be] animated by anything else than decency, generosity, moderation and consideration for others."
Such pride in purposes and steadiness in habits were
the foundation of Franklin's confidence that America would be a positive, potent, yet unmenacing force
in global destinies.

Edmund Burke once observed that for evil to
triumph in the world it required only that enough
good men do nothing. In a way this expresses the
essence of Franklin's public philosophy and outlook
on life. He had an intense interest in molding *good
men* and he believed profoundly that they *had an
obligation to act* for the common weal. In admiring
the example of his own father, in remembering the
lessons of *Pilgrim's Progress,* and in spreading
the useful folklore of Poor Richard throughout
America, he testified to his concern that men know
standards of good conduct and be able to translate
them into the precepts and habits of everyday life.

The Academy and the Hospital of Philadelphia are monuments to his conviction that impulses to do good can and must express themselves in institutions for promoting human welfare. The easy mixture of theory and application in his scientific work shows the restlessness of his mind both to know and to benefit mankind; it would not have occurred to him to separate the endeavors.

Franklin entered politics in part to restrain what he considered was the evil influence of the proprietary family in the affairs of Pennsylvania, and his dynamic concept of the British Empire had as its foundation a faith in the virtue of spreading growth-and-progress-in-freedom across the continent and around the globe. He worked diligently at Independence Hall in 1776 and 1787 because he thought it necessary for earnest men to act together, constructively and purposefully, both to repel evil measures and to construct a frame of government able to capitalize on the best, not the worst, in men. Most valuable of Franklin's contributions to the United States, then, was his testimony in word and deed that personal and political values were closely entwined and that thus connected they offered abundant opportunity for effective action on behalf of the general welfare. One wonders if any new nation could have had a more useful example and preceptor.

When news of Franklin's death in his eighty-fifth year (on April 17, 1790) spread around the world, the learned and the great of many nations paused to reflect on the meaning of the life and thought of this somehow uniquely significant individual. In France, full of the hope and the excitement of the first year of its Revolution, the passing of the man who more than any other person embodied the Enlightenment and who had won the heart of France during a long residence there, seemed especially noteworthy and poignant. Speaking before the French Academy of Sciences, of which Franklin had long been an honored member, Condorcet remarked on the special quality of Franklin's political thought:

> Franklin had not formed a general system of politics; he examined questions in proportion as the order of events or his foresight presented them to his mind, and he resolved them with the principles which he drew from a pure mind and in a just and acute spirit. In general he appeared not to seek to give the greatest degree of perfection to human institutions all at once; he believed it more certain to wait the passage of time; he did not insist upon delivering a frontal attack upon abuses, but found it more prudent first to attack the errors which are their source. He had in politics as in morality this type of indulgence which demands little because it hopes much and which pardons at the present in favor of the future. . . . In a word, his politics was that of a man who believed in the power of reason and the reality of virtue and who had wished to make himself teacher of his fellow citizens before being called to be their legislator.

This attitude, of course, was perfectly consistent with the character Franklin had given Poor Richard sixty years earlier, and was the hallmark of his forty-year career in public life.

To emphasize Franklin's role as patient preceptor and skillful tactician in politics, other eulogists pointed out, without seeing these traits as characteristic of his larger outlook on life, would be to miss his encompassing, harmonious personality. As much perhaps as any man who ever lived, he saw life whole. It would not have occurred to him to put science and politics, business and community welfare, morality and wit, or religion and education, in separate compartments. Reflecting about his long-time friend, the French scientist Jean-Baptiste Le Roy summarized what he saw as the essential feature of Franklin's mind:

... he had a particular characteristic which has not been sufficiently noticed, which was of always considering in any circumstance the most simple point of view. In his philosophical and political views, he always seized in every question the simplest aspect. If it was an explanation in natural philosophy, he did the same thing. In the arrangement of a machine, it was the same procedure. Whereas the generality of men arrive at the true and the simple only after a long circuit and multiplied efforts, his excellent mind, by a happy privilege, led him to the simplest means to explain the arranged phenomenon, to construct the apparatus which he needed, finally, to find the expedients the most proper to bring to a successful conclusion the projects or commissions with which he was charged.*

Franklin's capacity to keep his eye and mind on the simple essence of things, though, arose not from a habit of zealous singlemindedness but from an ability to sift and balance the abundant fruits of his endless curiosity. In a "eulogy" pronounced nearly a century and a half after those of Franklin's French admirers, his greatest biographer, Carl Van Doren, included this insight in what is still the most incisive comment on the significance of Philadelphia's first citizen:

Franklin's powers were from first to last in a flexible equilibrium. Even his genius could not

---

* Alfred Owen Aldridge, *Benjamin Franklin and His French Contemporaries* (New York, 1957), pp. 222-27, quotes these and other eulogies of Franklin in France.

specialize him. He moved through his world in
a humorous mastery of it. Kind as he was, there
was perhaps a little contempt in his lack of
exigency. He could not put so high a value as
single-minded men put on the things they give
their lives for. Possessions were not worth that
much, nor achievements. Comfortable as Franklin's possessions and numerous as his achievements were, they were less than he was.
Whoever learns about his deeds remembers
longest the man who did them. And sometimes,
with his marvelous range, in spite of his personal tang, he seems to have been more than
any single man: a harmonious human multitude.*

To an age often unable to blend humor with hope,
to be detached yet concerned, or to sense a harmony
which *does* make the whole more than the sum of
the parts, Franklin's life and thought may be of
especial significance. He showed that steady habits,
belief in the simple virtues, and a boundless zeal to
learn do indeed make the man, that such a man
can indeed contribute a mighty leaven to his community, and that such a community, or an aggregate
of them, can indeed affect the destiny of the world.
In a way it is inappropriate to call the ideas which
guided such a life a "philosophy"; a systematic,
rigorously logical system of thought could not have
survived intact the repeated applications to the real
world upon which Franklin insisted. Yet his age
was perfectly correct in calling him "the eminent
Philosopher Dr. Franklin." With his range of mind,
his ceaselessly critical probing, his clairvoyant sense
of the heart of matters, and his ready application
of thought to deed, he was in fact the fulfillment of
the Socratic ideal. His age accepted him as its au-

* Carl Van Doren, *Benjamin Franklin* (New York, 1938),
p. 782.

thentic sage because he taught a virtue and wisdom relevant in the world in which he lived—and this was the more marvelous because he lived everywhere from the printing shop on Market Street to the court of Versailles. Franklin gave himself to the world and his world view to all mankind when he set down his fervent hope that the day would come when "a Philosopher may set his Foot anywhere on Earth, and say 'This is my Country.'"

# Selected Bibliography

A full bibliography of writings about Franklin and his thought would require a large volume; a bibliography of his times and of the influences on his thought would fill several volumes. The following annotated list includes only the most pertinent and useful works.

## FRANKLIN'S WRITINGS

LABAREE, LEONARD W., *et al.* (eds.). *The Papers of Benjamin Franklin.* 7 vols. (1706-58) to date. New Haven, 1959——. The standard edition which, when complete, will supersede all others. Includes all of Franklin's writings and, so far, all letters written to him. Fully annotated.

SMYTH, ALBERT H. (ed.). *The Writings of Benjamin Franklin.* 10 vols. New York, 1905-07. The best completed edition of Franklin's writings, still necessary for documents not yet printed in *The Papers of Benjamin Franklin.*

FARRAND, MAX (ed.). *Benjamin Franklin's Memoirs Parallel Text Edition.* Berkeley, 1949. Printed in parallel columns, the four significant sources for Franklin's autobiography; fullest study of textual problems.

LABAREE, LEONARD W., *et al.* (eds.). *The Autobi-*

*ography of Benjamin Franklin.* New Haven, 1964. The standard edition, richly annotated, placing the famous *Autobiography* for the first time in the full context of what is known of Franklin's life from other sources.

CRANE, VERNER W. (ed.). *Benjamin Franklin's Letters to the Press, 1758-1775.* Chapel Hill, 1950. Valuable for Franklin's political writings in England.

COHEN, I. BERNARD (ed.). *Benjamin Franklin's Experiments. A New Edition of Franklin's Experiments and Observations on Electricity.* Cambridge, Mass., 1941. Includes Franklin's most famous scientific writings and a full analysis by the editor of their significance.

VAN DOREN, CARL (ed.). *The Letters of Benjamin Franklin and Jane Mecom.* Princeton, 1950. An important series of letters between Franklin and his sister covering the sixty-five years of their adult lives.

AMACHER, RICHARD E. *Franklin's Wit and Folly: The Bagatelles.* New Brunswick, 1953. Useful collection of Franklin's humorous writings.

MOTT, FRANK L., and JORGENSON, CHESTER E. (eds.). *Benjamin Franklin: Representative Selections, with Introduction, Bibliography, and Notes.* New York, 1936. A comprehensive general selection of Franklin's writings with a full bibliography of older works about Franklin and his thought.

KETCHAM, RALPH L. (ed.). *The Political Thought of Benjamin Franklin.* Indianapolis, 1965. Full collection of Franklin's political writings drawn from his personal letters and from works he intended for publication.

WHARTON, FRANCIS (ed.). *The Revolutionary Diplomatic Correspondence of the United States.* 6 vols. Washington, 1889. Contains many letters on Franklin's diplomatic service in France not printed elsewhere.

## BIOGRAPHIES

VAN DOREN, CARL. *Benjamin Franklin.* New York, 1938. A superb, full-length biography indispensable to any serious study of Franklin's life and thought.

BECKER, CARL L. *Benjamin Franklin, A Biographical Sketch.* Ithaca, N.Y., 1946. First printed in the *Dictionary of American Biography.* An excellent brief study especially useful in assessing Franklin's place in eighteenth-century thought.

CRANE, VERNER W. *Benjamin Franklin and a Rising People.* Boston, 1954. A good study emphasizing politics and diplomacy by a distinguished Franklin scholar.

BRUCE, W. C. *Benjamin Franklin, Self-Revealed.* 2 vols. New York, 1917. Combines Franklin's own writings with incisive commentary to present a vivid picture of his genius and personality. Occasionally extravagant.

PARTON, JAMES. *Life and Times of Benjamin Franklin.* 2 vols. New York, 1865. A detailed study still useful in evoking the mood of Franklin's life and times.

## STUDIES OF FRANKLIN'S THOUGHT

a. Among the countless essays on Franklin's thought, the following are especially suggestive and useful:

ROSSITER, CLINTON. "Benjamin Franklin," *Seedtime of the Republic.* New York, 1953, pp. 281-312. Emphasizes Franklin's political thought.

MOTT, FRANK L., and JORGENSON, CHESTER E. "Introduction," *Benjamin Franklin: Representative Selections* . . . , New York, 1936, pp. xiii-cxli. Em-

phasizes Franklin's standing as an Enlightenment
thinker.

PARRINGTON, VERNON L. "Benjamin Franklin: Our
First Ambassador," *Main Currents in American
Thought: The Colonial Mind, 1620-1800.* New
York, 1927, 1954, pp. 166-81. Pictures Frank-
lin as an early American democrat.

KOCH, ADRIENNE. "Franklin and Pragmatic Wisdom," *Power, Morals, and the Founding Fathers.*
Ithaca, N.Y., 1961. Sees Franklin as a "pragmatic
humanist."

b. The following are the best and most important
recent studies of the aspects of Franklin's thought
suggested in the titles:

ALDRIDGE, ALFRED O. *Franklin and His French Contemporaries.* New York, 1957.

COHEN, I. BERNARD. *Franklin and Newton, An In-
quiry into Speculative Newtonian Experimental
Science and Franklin's Work in Electricity as an
Example Thereof.* Philadelphia, 1956.

PACE, ANTONIO. *Benjamin Franklin and Italy.* Philadelphia, 1958.

STOURZH, GERALD. *Benjamin Franklin and American
Foreign Policy.* Chicago, 1954.

c. Of the older studies, the following are still useful
for the information they draw together, but are
more or less superseded by recent discoveries and by
more perceptive comment in later works:

CAREY, LEWIS J. *Franklin's Economic Views.* Garden
City, N.Y., 1928.

EISELEN, M. R. *Franklin's Political Theories.* Garden
City, N.Y., 1928.

MACLAURIN, LOIS M. *Franklin's Vocabulary.* Garden
City, N.Y., 1928.

McMASTER, JOHN B. *Benjamin Franklin As a Man
of Letters.* Boston, 1887.

STIFLER, JAMES M. *The Religion of Benjamin Franklin.* New York, 1925.

THORP, F. N. (ed.). *Benjamin Franklin and the University of Pennsylvania.* Washington, 1893.
WOODY, THOMAS. *Educational Views of Benjamin Franklin.* New York, 1931.


## CRITICAL AND INTERPRETIVE STUDIES

The introduction to the *Autobiography* edited by Leonard W. Labaree and others, mentioned above, summarizes critical attention to the *Autobiography* and makes reference to the most important criticisms of Franklin's thought as expressed in the *Autobiography*.

SANFORD, CHARLES L. (ed.). *Benjamin Franklin and the American Character.* Boston, 1955. Reprints a judicious selection of comments on Franklin, including the famous assault by D. H. Lawrence in *Studies in Classic American Literature* (1923).
THE FRANKLIN INSTITUTE. *Meet Dr. Franklin.* Philadelphia, 1943. Essays by leading authorities, including Carl Van Doren and Robert E. Spiller, assessing various aspects of Franklin's career.

Of the older estimates of Franklin and his thought, the following are the most incisive and enduring:
JEFFREY, FRANCIS. Review of an early edition of Franklin's *Works* in *The Edinburgh Review,* VIII (1806), 328-41.
PARKER, THEODORE. "Benjamin Franklin," *Historic Americans.* Boston, 1908; written in 1858 and first printed in 1870.
SAINTE-BEUVE, CHARLES AUGUSTIN. *English Portraits.* New York, 1875.

Of the many recent critical essays on Franklin, the following are the most useful:

218     *Selected Bibliography*

BELL, WHITFIELD J., JR. "Benjamin Franklin As an American Hero," *Association of American Colleges Bulletin,* XLIII, No. 1 (March, 1957), 121-32.

LEVIN, DAVID. "The Autobiography of Benjamin Franklin: The Puritan Experimenter in Life and Art," *The Yale Review,* LIII, No. 2, (December, 1963), 258-75.

LUCAS, F. L. *The Art of Living, Four Eighteenth-Century Minds; Hume, Horace Walpole, Burke, and Benjamin Franklin.* New York, 1959.

MILES, RICHARD D. "The American Image of Benjamin Franklin," *American Quarterly,* IX (1957), 117-43.

SAYRE, ROBERT F. "The Worldly Franklin and the Provincial Critics," *Texas Studies in Literature and Language . . . ,* IV (1963), 512-24.

WARD, JOHN W. "Who Was Benjamin Franklin," *The American Scholar,* XXXII, No. 4 (Autumn, 1963), 541-53.

WEBER, MAX. *The Protestant Ethic and the Spirit of Capitalism.* Translated by Talcott Parsons. New York, 1930, pp. 47-78.

WRIGHT, LOUIS B. "Franklin's Legacy to the Gilded Age," *Virginia Quarterly Review,* XXII (1946), 271-84.

## FRANKLIN AND HIS AGE

Of the hundreds of works on England, colonial America, and the Enlightenment, the following are especially important in placing Franklin's thought in its proper setting:

BECKER, CARL. *The Declaration of Independence.* New York, 1922. Excellent summary of the political theory of the American Revolution.

BEMIS, SAMUEL F. *The Diplomacy of the American Revolution.* New York, 1935. The standard work on the subject.

BELJAME, ALEXANDER. *Men of Letters and the English Public in the Eighteenth Century.* Translated by E. O. Lorimer. London, 1948. Good account of the effect English writers, especially Joseph Addison, had on public opinion.

BRIDENBAUGH, CARL and JESSICA. *Rebels and Gentlemen: Philadelphia in the Age of Franklin.* New York, 1942. The best account of life in Franklin's adopted city in his day.

BOORSTIN, DANIEL J. *The Americans: The Colonial Experience.* New York, 1958. 'Emphasizes the uniquely formative quality of life in a new world.

HANNA, WILLIAM S. *Benjamin Franklin and Pennsylvania Politics.* Stanford, 1964. A useful though overdrawn portrait of Franklin as a supporter of the Quaker "oligarchy" in Pennsylvania.

HINDLE, BROOKE. *The Pursuit of Science in Revolutionary America, 1735-1789.* Chapel Hill, 1956. An excellent survey of the milieu in which Franklin did his scientific work.

JONES, HOWARD M. *America and French Culture, 1750-1848.* Chapel Hill, 1927. An incisive study in comparative culture in which Franklin played a leading role.

KETCHAM, RALPH L. "Conscience, War, and Politics in Pennsylvania, 1755-1757," *William and Mary Quarterly,* 3rd ser., XX, No. 3 (July, 1963), 416-39. A detailed account of an important crisis in Franklin's political career.

PALMER, ROBERT R. *The Age of Democratic Revolution.* Princeton, 1959. An excellent study of the crosscurrents of politics and ideas in Europe and America, 1760-90.

ROSSITER, CLINTON. *Seedtime of the Republic.* New York, 1953. The best study of "The Origin of the American Tradition of Political Liberty."

SHEPARD, WILLIAM R. *History of Proprietary Government in Pennsylvania.* New York, 1896. A sympathetic account of the government under which Franklin lived for most of his adult life; a useful antidote to Franklin's antiproprietary bias.

STEPHEN, LESLIE. *A History of English Thought in the Eighteenth Century.* 2. vols. London, 1902. Still the best survey of the subject.

THAYER, THEODORE. *Pennsylvania Politics and the Growth of Democracy, 1740-1776.* Harrisburg, 1963. A useful survey of Franklin's political context despite its overambitious attempt to make Franklin and his associates early American "democrats."

TOLLES, FREDERICK B. *Meeting House and Counting House: The Quaker Merchants of Colonial Philadelphia, 1682-1763.* Chapel Hill, 1948. Valuable for its insights into the business and religious life of the dominant group among whom Franklin lived for thirty-five years.

WINSLOW, OLA E. *John Bunyan.* New York, 1961. Excellent study of the intellectual climate of the England from which Franklin's family came.

WRIGHT, LOUIS B. *Middle-Class Culture in Elizabethan England.* Chapel Hill, 1935. Describes the vigorous bourgeois spirit which flourished in England before and during Franklin's day.

# Index

221

North, Lord (2nd Earl of Guilford), 109, 116, 126

*Observations and Experiments in Electricity,* 109
*Observations Concerning the Increase of Mankind,* 100-3, 155
Old South Church (Boston), xi, 5, 48

Pacifism of Quakers, 90-91, 157
Parker, Theodore, on Franklin, 61-62
Paper currency, 88-89
"Parable Against Persecution, A," 172-74
Peace, Franklin on, 156-61
Pemberton, Henry, 78
Penn, Thomas, 92-93, 108-9
  on Franklin, 91
Penn, William, 92
Pennsylvania
  defense of
    Braddock's expedition, 93
    voluntary militia, 90-91
  proprietory rule of, 92-97
    Franklin in London to seek relief from, xii, 108, 111, 114, 116
Pennsylvania, University of, 71-72, 163
Pennsylvania Assembly
  Franklin as printer to, xi, 88
  Franklin in
    as clerk, xi, 88
    defeated for re-election, xiii
    first elected, 90
    hospital bill in, 73
  as unicameral, 195
Pennsylvania fireplace, 78-79
*Pennsylvania Gazette, The,* xi, 89, 109
Pennsylvania Hospital, xii, 72-74
*Pennsylvania Journal,* 95
Philadelphia, Pa., 47, 63, 108
  dirty streets of, 74-75
  fire companies of, 68
  influence on Franklin of, 49-50
  Library Company of, 67-68
  Junto in, 165, 203
    formation of, 67
    Puritan influence and, 29-30, 47
  watch of, 68

Philadelphia Academy, xii, 71-72, 82
Philadelphia Contributorship, 68-69
Pierce, William, on Franklin, 186
Pitt, William (Lord Chatham), xiii, 112, 116, 128, 132, 133
  Franklin on, 113
*Plain Truth,* xii, 90
Plutarch's *Lives,* 9, 13-17
Poetry, Franklin and, 61
Political philosophy of Franklin, 193-207
  foreign policy, 153-62, 205-6
*Poor Richard's Almanac,* xi, xii, 57-58, 82, 107
  sayings of, 58, 60, 189
Population, Franklin on, 100-3
*Port Royal Logic or the Art of Thinking,* 37-38
Pratt, Charles, 112
President, limited to one term, 193
Priestley, Joseph, 86
Progress, Franklin's faith in, 86, 110, 199-200, 201
*Proposals Relating to the Education of Youth in Pennsylvania,* xii, 69-71
Protestantism (Puritanism)
  anti-Catholic sentiment of, 1-2, 7-8
  Franklin as example of, 64
  influence on Franklin of, 1-2, 5-8, 25, 44-45, 47-49, 66-67, 130-31
  *See also* Religion

Quakers
  oligarchy in Pennsylvania of, 92
  pacifism of, 90-91, 157

Ray, Catharine, Franklin's letters to, 135-36
Reading by Franklin, 9-45
  Bunyan, 9-12
  Burton, 9, 17-22
  "Cato's Letters," 40
  Cotton Mather, 29-30, 45
    *Essays to do Good,* 9, 29-30, 45
  Defoe, 25-28
  deistic writers, 41-44